fun & funky crochet

fun & funky crochet

Sophie Britten

COLLINS & BROWN

Collins & Brown
The Chrysalis Building
Bramley Road
London
W10 6SP

An imprint of **Chrysalis** Books Group plc

British Library Cataloguing-in-Publication Data:
A catalogue record for this book is available from
the British Library.

ISBN: 1-84340-279-3 .

Designed by Lotte Oldfield
Edited and pattern checked by Susan Huran
Indexed by Isobel Mclean

Reproduction by Mission Productions, Hong Kong
Printed and bound by SNP Leefung, China

contents

introduction

Crochet is one of the most versatile and rewarding crafts. Although there is some dispute, it is widely believed that the craft originated in France. The modern name derives directly from the old French word "croché," meaning hook. It is thought that crochet was practiced in the eighteenth century by French nuns, who took their craft to Ireland where it quickly became popular, especially for making the lace with which Irish crochet is now synonymous.

Not just for nuns, crochet is now more popular than ever before. Today's crochet is a far cry from the frilly doilies and lacy collars that were fashionable right up until the Victorian times. Crochet is young and fun, and has never been easier to do. *Fun & Funky Crochet* features over 25 patterns for unique clothes and accessories, plus loads of ideas for customizing your jackets, sweaters and jeans. It also includes the basic techniques and incorporates many of the traditional elements of the craft, while giving the projects a new twist to bring crochet right up to the minute.

It's easy to make original clothes and accessories. Crochet is marvellously versatile, for shaping or using textured stitches like bobbles, loops or ripples. There are lots of different ways you can customize your clothes with crochet, giving a new funky look to an old garment. A beginner can start creating almost straight away. Once you have learnt the basics and a few stitches, the possibilities are endless. Add flowers, motifs, patches, edges, cuffs, and collars, or simply crochet a design right onto your clothes. The book also explains how you can add beads and baubles (or anything that can be threaded onto the yarn) to make beaded edgings.

You don't have to be a designer or an expert to make these amazing things – all you need is a crochet hook and some yarn. So let *Fun & Funky Crochet* inspire you to learn this simple, but beautiful craft.

fantastic yarns

You can crochet with practically anything that has length and flexibility – if you had a large enough hook, and a big emergency, you could even crochet your bedsheets together.

But before you go that far, there are some truly fantastic yarns around that are just waiting to be picked up and turned into amazing creations.

Most crochet suppliers sell cotton crochet yarns, which are principally for lace-making and filet, and also a range of Goldfingering filet and yarn, which is a synthetic yarn woven through with metallic thread. It comes in a wide variety of colours, and I always make sure I have some gold or silver on sparkly trims to hats, jumpers, cardigans – anything and everything.

You can also crochet with any knitting yarns that are available in your local wool shop or haberdashers. As well as the traditional natural fibres such as wool and cotton, there are some really exciting mixed synthetic-and-natural and totally synthetic yarns. Recent years have seen a proliferation in multi-coloured, bobbled, textured, spangly and otherwise exotic yarns. And in general, one ball is enough to makeover an item of clothing or make a small accessory, such as a bag or hat. Still it never hurts to buy more than you think you'll need – shops will always refund what you don't use.

If you can't find what you're looking for in the shops, take a look online at some of the many mills or wholesalers selling all kinds of wools, synthetic yarns, ribbons, metallics and a wide choice of beautiful and hard-to-find natural wools, such as mohair (for a list of stockists see the back of the book). If you're just planning small projects, some mills sell bags of odds and discontinued ends of stock very cheaply.

tips & hints

Dye lots:
When buying more than one ball of a particular yarn, make sure the dye lot numbers printed on the ball band are the same, otherwise there may be a slight variation in colour.

Hook size:
Most yarns will tell you on the ball band what size knitting needle they recommend you use – for crochet you should use half a size or a whole size larger. The larger the hook, the larger the stitch and the looser your work will be.

Choosing yarns:
To ensure your crocheted article appears the same as in the pattern, you should use the yarn that is recommended. If you cannot find the same yarn, choose one of a similar weight and type and crochet a sample to check the tension and appearance.

Washing instructions:
Care instructions should be given on the ball band, however – where there are none or you are unsure, you should wash a sample first.

materials

Unlike many other crafts, crochet uses amazingly few materials. All you need to get started is some yarn and a crochet hook, although there are a few other items that will come in handy.

Tapestry needles:
Large blunt needles that are used for joining the seams together.

Tape measure:
This is indispensable for checking tension and when making fitted garments, as you will often need to measure the work.

Scissors:
They should be small and sharp for cutting yarn.

Crochet hook conversion chart:
Normal crochet hooks vary in size from 2mm to 15mm and are 15cm long. They are most commonly available in plastic and aluminium. The larger hooks will be plastic as this is lighter and easier to hold. You may have also come across steel hooks, these tend to be much smaller (less than 2 mm) and are used for intricate lace-making and filet work.

You may find that different pattern books use different systems to express the sizes. The chart on the right will help you to choose the correct hook.

METRIC SIZES (mm)	US SIZES	UK/ CANADIAN
2.0	–	14
2.25	B/1	13
2.5	–	12
2.75	C/2	–
3.0	–	11
3.25	D/3	10
3.5	E/4	9
3.75	F/5	–
4.0	G/6	8
4.5	7	7
5.0	H/8	6
5.5	I/9	5
6.0	J/10	4
6.5	K/10 1/2	3
7.0	–	2
8.0	L/11	0
9.0	M/13	00
10.0	N/15	000

following instructions

Crochet patterns use special terminology that is often abbreviated or shown as symbols on a chart. Becoming familiar with these will make your crocheting quicker and more enjoyable.

Before you start on any project, read through the instructions to make sure you understand all of the information. Where different sizes are given clearly mark which size you are going to make and highlight instructions for that size throughout the pattern. This will make it much easier to follow.

Where there is a recurring instruction, the start of the section of the pattern to be repeated is indicated with an asterisk, for example: *dc, ch 2, dc in 2 ch sp; repeat from * until last st.

Abbreviations

The table of abbreviations (right) lists the most common abbreviations and all those that are used in this book. However, it is not an exhaustive list as there are many different crochet stitches, not all of which are used in this book.

beg	Beginning
BLO	Back loop only
ch	Chain
ch sp	Chain space
cm	Centimetres
cont	Continue
dc	Double crochet
dec	Decrease
dtr	Double treble
FLO	Front loop only
foll	Following
in	Inches
inc	Increase
patt	Pattern
rem	Remaining
rep	Repeat
RS	Right side
sp	Space
ss	Slip stitch
st(s)	Stitch(es)
tch	Turning chain
tog	Together
tr	Treble
trtr	Triple treble
WS	Wrong side
yrh	Yarn round hook

Charts

A chart is often used in filet crochet. It is based on a square grid, in which vertical lines represent treble stitches and horizontal lines represent chains. Patterns are created by filling in some of the squares; where a square is filled with a dot, a chain is replaced by a treble.

Charts can also be used to give directions for colour patterns.

Tension

This is the number of rows and stitches per centimetre or inch, usually measured over 10 square cm (4 in). The tension will determine the size of the finished item. The correct tension is given at the beginning of each pattern. Crochet a small swatch using the recommended yarn and hook to make sure you are working to the correct tension. If your work is too loose, choose a hook that is one size smaller, and if it is too tight, choose a hook the next size up. When making clothes it is important to check your tension before you start; it is not worth making something the wrong size. When measuring work, lay it on a flat surface and always measure at the centre, rather than the side edges.

The good news is that few of the patterns in this book require you to work to an exact tension, however it is important to be consistent in order to make a nice even fabric that is neither too tight, nor too loose. The advantage of working with fluffy, furry and other textured yarns is that minor inconsistencies won't show.

To keep your tension even it is a good idea to have a piece of scrap crochet on hand to warm up each time you pick up your work.

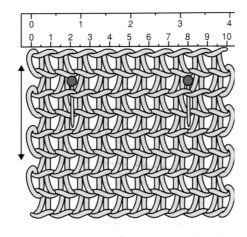

tips & hints

- If you are making a large number of base chains, it is worth leaving a long tail when you start, so that if you find on your first row that you haven't done enough chains, you can undo the slip knot and create a few more. Similarly, don't worry if you have done too many chains, as these can usually be sewn in at the end.

- Always finish the row or round you are working on to avoid losing your place in the pattern.

- Unless the pattern says otherwise, always join a new ball of yarn at the end of a row, not in the middle. This way, it can be neatly sewn in afterwards.

- Always turn the work clockwise to avoid twisting your stitches.

learning to crochet

Crochet is a relatively simple and hugely rewarding way of making clothes, accessories and household items with wonderful textures.

Crochet is made up from a series of interlocking loops. Unlike knitting, each stitch is completed before working the next, so after each stitch you are left with only one loop of yarn on your hook. The advantage of working one complete stitch at a time is that you avoid the risk of dropping stitches.

Crochet is easy to learn and once you have mastered the basics, you will be able to make a wide variety of wonderful items.

First you will need a crochet hook: a 4 or 5mm one is a good choice for beginners. As for yarns, it will be easier to see what you are doing if you use a smooth yarn, so avoid working with any yarns that are too fluffy (like mohair), until you become more confident.

Holding the hook

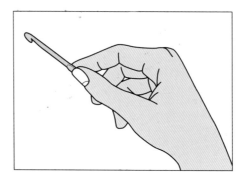

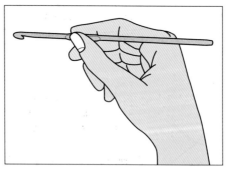

If you are right-handed hold the hook like a knife in your right hand (see above top). You can also hold the hook like a pencil (see above), if you find that more comfortable.

Controlling your yarn

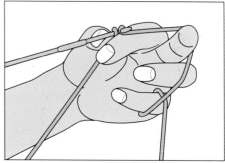

Wrap the yarn around your little finger and over the third, second and index fingers as shown. Extend the second/middle finger to control the yarn and hold the work firmly between the thumb and index finger.

If you are left-handed, you should hold the hook in your left hand and the yarn in your right. Reverse the instructions. It may be helpful to prop up the book in front of a mirror.

Getting started

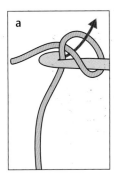 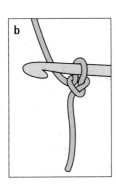 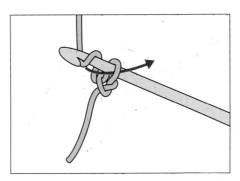

Start off by making a slipknot: make a loop near the end of the yarn; then insert the hook into the loop from front to back and draw another loop through it (a). Pull the knot close to the hook, but not too tight (b).

Now you are ready to crochet. Most crochet starts with a base chain, which is a series of chain stitches.

To make a chain (ch), wrap the yarn round the hook from back to front (this is called yarn round hook, or yrh) and draw it through the loop on the hook (above left). This makes one chain stitch.

If you are completely new to crochet, practice making chains until you have a smooth action and can easily make even chains of the same size.

tips & hints

- There should be just one loop left on the hook at the completion of a stitch.

- **Always** insert the hook into the stitch from front to back, unless the pattern says otherwise.

- **Always** insert the hook under the top two loops on chain or stitch, unless the pattern says otherwise.

- When counting chains, do not include the loop on the hook.

basic stitches

Start by making a series of chains, around 10 will be enough. Now you're ready to practise the following stitches.

Slip stitch (ss)

Double crochet (dc)

This is the shortest stitch and in fact lies flat to the work. It mostly used for joining and shaping. Insert the hook into a stitch or chain (always remember to insert the hook under both strands of the stitch), yarn round hook from the back to the front of the hook, now draw the hook through the stitch and the loop on the hook. You are left with just one loop on the hook. This is one slip stitch.

This is the most common and shortest fabric-making stitch. It creates a compact fabric that is worked forward and backward in rows.

Insert the hook into the second chain from the hook, yarn round hook, draw the loop through your work (a), yarn round hook and draw the hook through both loops on the hook (b). You are left

with one loop on the hook. This is one double crochet. Repeat into the next stitch or chain. Work until the very last chain. This is one row of double crochet. At the end of the row, make one chain stitch – this is your turning chain – turn the work and work one dc into each stitch of the previous row, ensuring you insert the hook under both loops of the stitch you are crocheting into.

Half treble (htr)

Treble (tr)

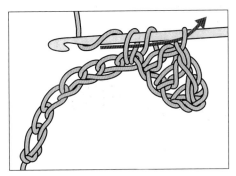

This stitch is similar to double crochet, but taller. So yarn round hook before inserting the hook into the third chain from the hook, yarn round hook, draw one loop through the work, yarn round hook, draw through all three loops on the hook, leaving just one loop on the hook. This is one half treble.

When you reach the end of the row, make two chains – this counts as the first stitch of the next row. Turn the work, and continue, missing the first htr of the previous row. At the end of the row work the last half treble into the top of the turning chain of the row below.

This stitch is taller yet. As with the half treble, start by wrapping the yarn around the hook and insert the hook into the fourth chain from the hook, yarn round hook, draw one loop through the work (a), yarn round hook, draw through the first two loops on the hook, yarn round hook, draw through the remaining two loops on the hook (b), leaving just one loop on the hook. This is one treble.

When you reach the end of the row, make three chains. These count as the first stitch of the next row. Turn the work and miss the first treble of the previous row; insert the hook into the second stitch of the new row. Continue to work until the end of the row, inserting the last treble into the top of the turning chain of the row below.

basic techniques

As well as working from right to left in rows, you can also work in the round, either complete rounds or as a continuous spiral. This a great way of making seamless items and is an essential technique for making hats, bags and other rounded objects.

Making fabric – working in rows

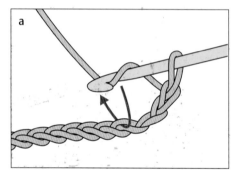

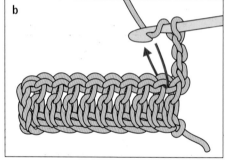

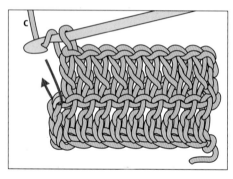

To make a flat fabric in crochet, as with knitting, you work to and fro in rows.

First make as many chain stitches as you require. This row is called the base chain. To allow for the height of the stitch, insert the hook into the 2nd chain from the hook (not counting the chain on the hook) for double crochet, 4th chain from the hook for treble crochet (a), and so on.

Work from right to left inserting the hook under two of the three threads in each chain.

At the end of the row, turn the work (remember always to turn your work in the same direction).

When you reach the end of the row, you need to work a turning chain. This is one or more chains, depending on the height of the stitch. Turning chains should be worked as follows:

Double crochet: 1 chain
Half treble: 2 chains
Treble: 3 chains
Double treble: 4 chains
Triple treble: 5 chains

Now turn the work to begin working on the next row. When working in double crochet, insert the hook into the first stitch in the new row and work each stitch to the end of the row, excluding the turning chain. For all other stitches, unless the pattern states otherwise, the turning chain counts as the first stitch, miss 1 stitch (b) and work each stitch to the end of the row including the top of the turning chain (c).

Working in the round

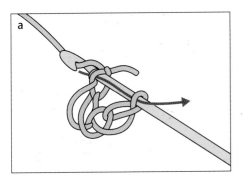

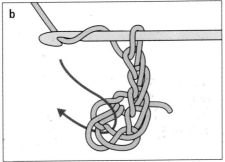

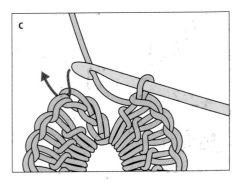

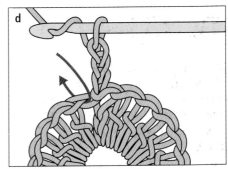

Crochet in the round starts with a ring. To make a ring, make a series of chains and join the last chain to the first with a slip stitch (a). To make the first round, work a starting chain to the height of the stitch you are working in (eg. double crochet – 1 chain, treble crochet – 3 chains etc.), then work as many stitches as you need into the centre of the ring (b) and finish the round with a slipstitch into the first stitch (c).

Begin the second and subsequent rounds with a starting chain, then insert the hook under the top two loops of each stitch in the previous round (d). At the end of the round, join to the top of the starting chain with a slip stitch.

Changing colours

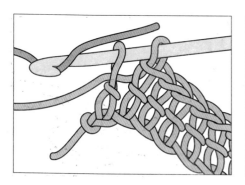

The patterns in this book will only require you to change colour at the end of the row or round. To do this, change yarns during the last st in the row, by working the last loop of the st before you need to change yarn using the new yarn so the new colour is ready to be used for the turning chain. If you are going to use the original colour again in a few rows, don't cut the yarn, but carry it up the side or the back if you are working in rounds.

Increasing

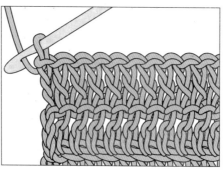

Shaping
As with knitting, fabric is most often shaped by increasing or decreasing the number of stitches in a row or round.

Increasing
To increase, simply work an additional stitch into the next stitch. A single increase is made by working 2 stitches into the same stitch. You can of course increase by more than one stitch at a time.

Bobble

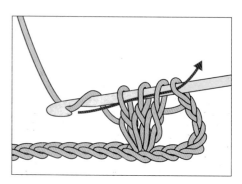

Bobble
This method of working several stitches in the same place can also be used to create interesting textures such as bobbles, which are two or more stitches worked into the same stitch and joined together at the top.

Decreasing

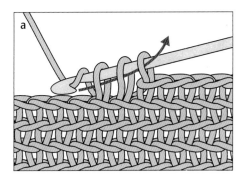 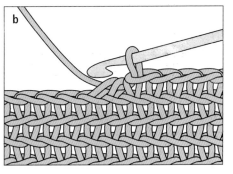 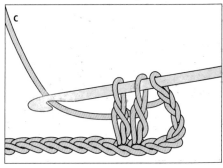

dc2tog

To decrease, two or more stitches are worked together. To decrease 1 stitch in double crochet (dc2tog), insert hook into the next st, yarn round hook, draw through a loop, insert hook into the next st, yrh, draw through a loop, yrh, draw through all three loops, leaving just one loop.

dc3tog

To decrease by two stitches in double crochet work 3 stitches together (dc3tog) by working as for dc2tog until you have three loops on the hook, insert the hook into the next st, yrh, draw through a loop, yrh and draw through all four loops.

tr2tog

To decrease 1 stitch in treble crochet (tr2tog), yrh, insert hook into the next stitch, yrh, draw through the work, yrh, draw through 2 loops, yrh, insert hook into next st, yrh, draw through the work, yrh, draw through 2 loops, yrh, draw through all three loops, leaving just one loop.

finishing off

The finish is an important part of making a project, so don't be tempted to rush the final stages. Time and care are essential for a neat and tidy finish, especially when joining pieces together.

Fastening off

Cut the yarn to roughly 13 cm (5 in), (if you are going to be sewing up a seam you should leave a longer tail). Draw the tail through the loop on the hook and pull firmly. Weave the end an inch or a few centimetres in one direction and then back the other way for a neat and secure finish.

Pressing

Where the pattern requires you to press your work, place the item under a piece of damp cloth and iron flat. Goldfingering items will benefit especially from pressing, whereas fluffy yarns and textured stitches, such as loop stitch, should be left so as not to spoil the look of the fabric.

Seams

There are various ways of sewing up seams. Two principal methods are given here: joining the seams edge-to-edge using flat stitch and slipstitch seams. Flat stitch creates an almost invisible, ridgeless seam. Slipstitch is stronger, and most suited to seams where minimal stretch is required.

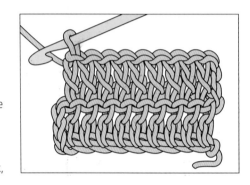

To fasten off, cut the yarn, draw the tail through the loop on the hook and pull firmly.

tips & hints

- For all sewing use a blunt-tipped tapestry needle that won't split yarn.

Slip stitch

This seam uses a crochet hook and creates a very firm join, suitable for bags or other items that do not need much flexibility.

With the right sides together, insert the hook into the first stitch of both sections, yarn round hook, draw the loop through both stitches and the loop on the hook. Repeat along the length of the seam.

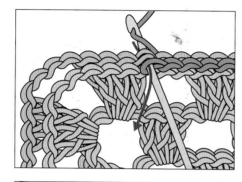

Flat stitch

This seam is sewn with a tapestry needle and creates an almost invisible join. It is used when the number of stitches is the same on both pieces. Lay the two sections right side up with the stitches aligned. Insert the needle under the lower half of the edge st on one section, then under the upper half of the edge st on the opposite section. Repeat along the length of the seam.

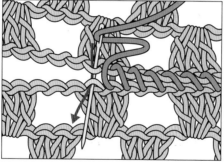

flowers and motifs

Crochet is a great way to customize your clothes. Adding decorative motifs is a fun way of revamping an old garment, adding to a new one or simply making a change.

Learn how to make flowers, fruit and other simple motifs that can be sewn or even just pinned onto existing clothes or shoes. Most of the ideas in this section require only very small quantities of yarn, so it's a great way to use up any odds and ends you may have left from other projects.

Once you've mastered a few of the basic techniques shown here, the possibilities are limitless!

Motifs are generally symmetrical designs that can be used individually (as we are doing here) or used in multiples and sewn together to create patchworks and other items. Because they're so quick to make and use very little yarn, they are a great way of customizing your clothes easily and cheaply.

Here are four simple motifs that can be sewn directly onto your clothes or used with a pin to make a brooch.

Daisy

A simple and versatile daisy motif with petals made of chain stitches.

Materials
Rowan Cotton Glace in Hyacinth
3.5 mm crochet hook

Make 6 ch and join in a ring with a ss.
Round 1: Work 14 dc into ring, ss to 1st dc at beg of round to close.
Round 2: Work (1 dc, 6 ch, 1 dc) into front loop only of each dc. Ss to 1st dc to close.
Round 3: Work (1 dc, 8 ch, 1 dc) into back loop only of each dc, ss to 1st dc to close.

Fasten off.
You can either attach a brooch pin to the back or simply use a safety pin.

Rose

An easy three dimensional rose that can be worn on a hat, bag, jacket, jeans…anywhere!

Materials
Rowan Cotton Glace in Candy Floss
3.5 mm crochet hook
Make 8 ch and join into a ring with a ss.

Round 1: 6 ch (count as 3 ch and 1 tr),*1 tr into ring, 3 ch; repeat from * 4 more times, ss into 3rd of 6 ch.
Round 2: Work 1 petal (1dc, 1 htr, 3tr, 1htr, 1dc) into each 3 ch sp.
Round 3: *5 ch, 1 dc into last dc of next petal; repeat from * ending with 5 ch.
Round 4: Work 1 petal (1dc, 1 htr, 5tr, 1htr, 1dc) into each 5 ch sp.
Round 5: *7 ch, 1 dc into last dc of next petal; repeat from * ending with 7 ch.
Round 6: Work 1 petal (1dc, 1 htr, 7tr, 1htr 1dc) into each 7 ch sp, ss to 1st dc.
Fasten off.

Left: A contrasting daisy stitched to a bikini bottom.

Opposite: A rose worn as a brooch.

Cherries

A simple and bold design – these three-dimensional cherries look almost good enough to eat!
They would look fantastic sewn onto a hat or jacket or suspended from a brooch.

Materials

Rowan Cotton Glace in Poppy and Shoot
3.5 mm crochet hook

Special abbreviation

dtr: double treble – yrh twice, insert hook into work, yrh, draw through work, yrh, draw through first 2 loops, yrh, draw through next 2 loops, yrh, draw through last 2 loops.

Fruit – make two

Make 4 ch.
Row 1: 8 dtr into 4th ch from hook, turn.
Row 2: 3 ch, *leaving last loop of each dtr on hook, work 1 dtr into each of next 4 dtr, yrh, draw through all 5 loops on hook; repeat from * once more.
Fasten off.

Leaves
First leaf

Make 10 ch.
Round 1: 1 dc into 2nd ch from hook, 1 htr into next ch, 1 tr into each of next 3 ch, work 1 dtr into next ch, 1 tr into next ch, 1 htr into next ch, 1 dc into last ch. 1 ch. Don't turn
Round 2: 1 dc into back of each ch, work (1 dc, 1ch, 1dc) into tch, 1 dc into each st to end. ss into starting ch. Do not fasten off.

Second leaf

Make 10 ch.
Round 1: 1 dc into 2nd ch from hook, 1 htr into next ch, 1 tr into each of next 3 ch, work 1 dtr into next ch, 1 tr into next ch, 1 htr into next ch, 1 dc into last ch. 1 ch, turn.
Round 2: 1 dc into each st, work (1 dc, 1 ch, 1dc) into tch, 1 dc into back of each ch to last but one ch, ss into last ch. Fasten off.
Use brown or black yarn of a similar weight to attach the cherries to the leaves with a series of chains.

Star

This star is easy to make. It can be worn individually or can be made into an interesting patchwork fabric by making lots of identical stars and sewing them together.

Materials

Rowan Cotton Glace in Zeal
3.5 mm crochet hook

Special abbreviation

dtr: double treble – yrh twice, insert hook into work, yrh, draw through work, yrh, draw through first 2 loops, yrh, draw through next 2 loops, yrh, draw through last 2 loops.

Make 2 ch.
Round 1: 5 dc into 2nd ch from hook.
Round 2: 3 dc into each dc.
Round 3: *1 dc into next st, 6 ch, ss in 2nd ch from hook, 1 dc into next ch, 1 htr into next ch, 1 tr into next ch, 1 dtr into next ch, 1 dtr into base of starting dc, miss 2 dc; repeat from * 4 more times. Ss into 1st dc to join.
Round 4: *1 dc into each ch, (1 dc, 1 ch, 1dc) into tch, 1 dc into each of next 6 sts, ss into next dc; repeat from * 4 more times.
Fasten off.

edgings and inserts

Crochet is the ideal way to add edgings to the cuffs or hem of an old cardigan or a plain jumper that needs enlivening. Here are five funky edgings to add pizzazz to your clothes!

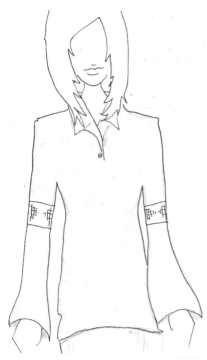

If you are crocheting directly onto your clothes, use a yarn that is of a similar weight to the garment you are customizing. If the weight of the yarn and size of the stitches differs greatly, work 1 row of dc of an intermediate weight yarn around the edge to create an even base for your decorative trim. To add edgings to woven fabrics, make the trimming first and sew it on afterwards.

Crab stitch border

This is a very simple border using double crochet worked from left to right, instead of right to left as normal. It can be worked on any number of sts and is a good way of finishing off a crocheted item, especially if you use a contrasting colour.

Join yarn at the seam. Working from left to right, insert hook into next st, yarn round hook, draw through a loop, yrh, draw through both loops. Fasten off.

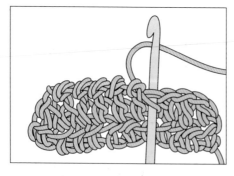

Above left: Crochet insert in the sleeves of a cotton tunic.

Shell border

This is a very simple but effective border which creates a pretty shell effect on a knitted or crocheted garment, especially on a cuff or hem.

Join the yarn at a seam, and work one row of dc
  evenly around the edge of the fabric.
Make sure the final number of sts is a multiple of 6
  (add 2 ch if working separate trimming).
Join with a ss to 1st dc.
*Miss 2 sts, 5 tr into next st, miss 2 sts, 1 ss into
  next st; repeat from * to end, ss to ss at beg.
Fasten off.

Right: The shell border has an attractive scalloped edge.
Far right: Picot border.

Picot border

This is a very pretty edging for a demure sweetheart look!

Join the yarn at a seam, and work one row
of dc evenly around the edge of the fabric.
Make sure the final number of sts is a multiple of 3
  (add 2 ch if working separate trimming).
Join with a ss to 1st dc.
*1 ss into each of next 2 sts, 1 dc into next st, 3
  ch, 1 dc in same st as last dc; repeat from * to
  end, ss into 1st st. Fasten off.

Arches border

A fun lacy border with two rows of arches. This is great for adding a bit of length to a cuff or hem.

Join the yarn at a seam, and work one row of dc evenly around the edge of the fabric. Make sure the final number of sts is a multiple of 7 plus 1 (add 3 ch if working separate trimming). Join with a ss to 1st dc.

Round 1: 3 ch (count as 1 tr), miss 1 dc, 1 tr into each dc to end, ss into top of tch.

Round 2: 1 ch, 1 dc into each of first 2 tr, *7ch, miss 4 tr, 1 dc into each of next 3 tr; repeat from * to end, omitting 1 dc at end of last repeat, ss into 1st dc.

Round 3: 1 ch, 1 dc into each of first 2 dc, *7dc into 7 ch sp, 1 dc into each of next 3 dc; repeat from * to end omitting 1 dc at end of last repeat, ss into 1st dc.

Round 4: 7 ch (count as 1 dtr, 3 ch), miss 4 dc, 1 dc into each of next 3 dc, *7 ch, miss 7 dc, 1 dc into each of next 3 dc; repeat from * to last 4 dc, 3 ch, 1 dtr into last dc, ss to 4th ch of 7 ch.

Round 5: 1 ch, 3 dc into 3 ch sp,*1 dc into each of next 3 dc, 7 dc into 7 ch sp, repeat from * to end, working 3 dc into last 3 ch sp, ss into 1st dc. Fasten off.

Frills and spills

Here's a really quick and easy way of making an unusual trimming using fronds of chains worked first into the front then into the back of a row of double crochet.

Join the yarn at a seam, and work one row of dc evenly around the edge of the fabric. Any number of stitches will work with this trim. Join with a ss to 1st dc.

Round 1: *7 ch, ss into the front loop only of the next st; repeat from * to end.

Round 2: *7 ch, ss into the back loop only of the next st; repeat from * to end, ss into 1st st. Fasten off.

Left: Arches border.

Right: Frilly chains border.

Filet insert

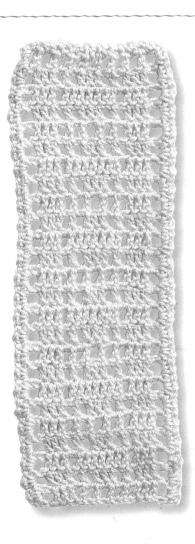

Filet is an ancient and traditional method of making decorative edgings. This section explains how, using a fine yarn, you can make pretty and interesting bands of filet crochet to insert into a sleeve or bodice.

The principle of filet crochet is that it is made from a network of treble and chain sts. You can make interesting patterns using open squares and blocks (shown by dots on the chart). Use a sheet of graph paper to plot your pattern: in each blank square a treble is missed and a chain worked, in each blocked square a treble is worked into every stitch.

You can either follow the pattern pictured left or make your own design. Simple symmetrical designs will work best. And unless you are using a very fine yarn the band should be no more than 10 squares wide. When calculating the length of base ch, work on number of squares x 2 + 3 (count as 1st treble).

To make the insert shown here:
Make 21 ch, 1 tr into 5th ch from hook, *1 ch, miss 1 ch, 1 st into next ch; repeat from * to end. For each empty square work 1 ch, miss 1 tr, 1 tr into next st, for each filled square, work 1 tr into each st, (including ch). Work last tr into 3rd of 4 ch.

Follow the pattern until the band is the correct length for the garment into which you wish to insert it. Fasten off.

Edging
To give the insert a pretty finish, work a picot border round each of the long edges as follows: Work (1 dc, 1 ch, 1 dc) into each row end.

Making up
To attach your insert, sew one side by hand or machine to the edge of your garment, then with the wrong side facing, sew up your band seam, and finally sew the other edge to the other edge of your garment.

Left: A filet insert band, with an example of a filet chart.

collars and cuffs

Surface crochet is the method of adding texture to knitted or crocheted fabric. It can be used to add interest to cuffs and collars as we've done here, or to apply motifs and patterns to a knitted or crocheted garment for a radical new look.

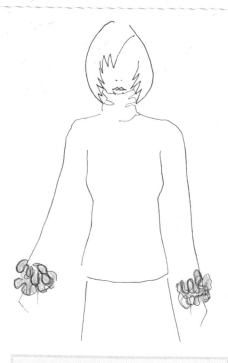

Opposite: Some of the great cuffs you can crochet – some of which would also work well as an edging round the neckline too! Clockwise, from bottom left – Bahamas Palm Fronds, Amazing Yarn – frilly edge, Raised Wave Cuff and Midas Ribs.

tips & hints

• If the yarn used in the fabric you are working into is much finer than the yarn you are customizing with, you can work a row of dc round the edge of the cuff or collar in an intermediate weight yarn.

Bahamas Palm Fronds

Add a tropical touch to your clothes with this spike stitch border.

Materials
Rowan Cotton Glace in Shoot
3.5 mm crochet hook

Round 1: 1 ch, work a round of dc evenly around edge, ensuring the final number of sts is a multiple of 4, ss to 1st ch.

Round 2: 1 ch, 1 dc into each of first 2 sts, *insert hook into fabric to the right of the next st, pick up yarn and draw up to height of edge, work directly below and to theleft in the same way, insert hook into next st, yrh,draw loop through, yrh, draw through all 5 loops, 1 dc into each of next 3 sts; repeat from * to end, ss to 1st ch.
Fasten off. Sew in all ends.

Amazing Yarn – frilly edge

With the really interesting yarns out there you can make radical changes with simple techniques.

Materials
Sirdar Fizz in Carnival
3.5 mm crochet hook

Round 1: 1 ch, work a round of dc evenly around edge so that you are left with an odd number of sts, ss to 1st ch to join.

Round 2: *6 ch, miss next dc, 1 dc into next dc; repeat from * to end.

Round 3: 3 ch, * 1 dc into 6 ch space, 6 ch; repeat from * to end, working last dc into 3 ch space. Fasten off.

Raised Wave Cuff

This trim is worked in two tiers to stand out from the cuff. This works with any multiple of 7 dc.

Materials
Rowan Cotton Glace in Poppy
3.5 mm crochet hook

Round 1: Work 1 st into each dc as follows: *1 dc, 1 htr, 1 tr, 1 dtr, 1 tr, 1 htr, 1 dc; repeat from * to end.

Round 2: Work 1 st into each st of Round 1:

*1 dc, 1 htr, 1 tr, 1 dtr, 1 tr, 1 htr, 1 dc;
repeat from * to end.

Round 3: Work 1 st into the base of each st of
Round 1: *1 dc, 1 htr, 1 tr, 1 dtr, 1 tr, 1 htr, 1 dc;
repeat from * to end.

Round 4: Work 1 st into each st of Round 3: *1 dc,
1 htr, 1 tr, 1 dtr, 1 tr, 1 htr, 1 dc;
repeat from * to end. Fasten off.
Open out the two tiers and press flat.

Midas Ribs

Goldfingering yarn worked onto the surface of cuffs
in ribs of uneven length creates a glamorous gilded
edge. Working double crochet into the surface of
the fabric is no different to regular double crochet:
insert the hook into the fabric from front to back
and then from back to front, so the hook emerges
a short distance from where it went in (this will be
the length of the stitch), yrh, draw loop through
fabric, yrh, draw through remaining 2 loops.

Materials
2 mm crochet hook
Goldfingering yarn in gold (Note: all Goldfingering
yarn used in the book is manufactured by Twilleys.)

Round 1: 1 ch, work dc around the cuff edge so
that the final number of sts is a multiple of 4, ss
to first dc.

Round 2: 1 dc into first dc, * work a row of dc into

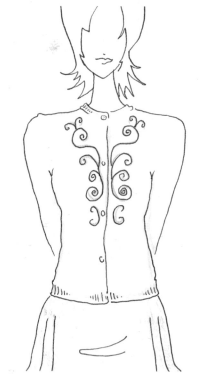

the fabric perpendicular to cuff edge, say 8 sts,
turn, miss 1st dc, 1 dc into each dc until you reach
cuff edge, 1 dc into each of next 3 dc along cuff
edge; repeat from * working a different number of
stitches for each rib, ss into first dc.

Round 3: 1 ch, 1 dc into each dc around cuff edge,
ss into 1st dc. Fasten off.
Sew in all ends.

Crochet collars

There are many possiblities with crochet – use any of
the edgings or cuff suggestions to liven up a dull
neckline, or for a purely decorative effect, surface
crochet can be used to create any pattern you like.
To achieve the best results, when crocheting onto
a pre-made knitted or crocheted garment, select a
yarn that is similar in weight to that used in the
fabric. If the knit is very fine, as is shown here, you
should also use a fine yarn and a small hook;
otherwise you will not be able to draw the hook
and the yarn through the fabric.

Materials
2 mm crochet hook
Rowan Kid Silk Haze in Marmalade

First, decide on your design, if it is complicated or
requires symmetry, use a dressmaker's pencil to
mark your design directly onto the fabric.

Thread the yarn through from the back to the front
of the garment, so that the tail is at the back and
the ball at the front. Insert hook into and back out
of the fabric and draw through a loop, yrh hook,
draw through two loops. Continue to work in this
way, following the pencil markings (or you could go
freestyle and work where your hook takes you!). If
you are using a very fine yarn, you might want to
work 2 or 3 rows so your design really stands out.

patches and pockets

Four funky pockets or patches that can be stitched anywhere and onto anything! Add interest and colour to your jeans, brighten up a dull bag – or even join several patches together to make a cushion or a small throw.

Two of these designs use colour, the first in a traditional square motif, known as a granny square. Individually these can be used to make pockets (or items such as placemats), but sewn together, they can also be used in multiples to make much larger items, like a patchwork quilt or, as is shown later on in the book, to make a granny squares scarf. The second uses two colours to make zigzag stripes.

The other two pockets use textured stitches: one a busy bobbly pocket and the other an ingenious way of making crochet fur. All the pockets can be made in any size with any yarn. The materials used here are just a guideline – let your imagination run free!

Above: A traditional square motif, known as a granny square.

Multi-coloured granny square

For a bright pocket or patch for your jeans, this is a fun and bold design using 6 colours. It's a great way to use up odds and ends of yarn. Remember, the thicker the yarn, the bigger the patch!

Special abbreviation

dtr: double treble – yrh twice, insert hook into work, yrh, draw through work, yrh, draw through first 2 loops, yrh, draw through next 2 loops, yrh, draw through last 2 loops.

Materials

A small quantity of Rowan Cotton Glace in 6 different colours
3.5 mm crochet hook

Using colour A, make 4 ch, join into a ring with a ss into 1st ch.

Round 1: 4 ch, 3 dtr into ring (2 ch, 4 dtr into ring) 3 times, 2 ch, ss to 4th of 1st 4 ch. Break off A and turn.

Round 2: Join colour B to next 2 ch sp, 2 dc into same space * 1 dc into each of next 4 sts, [2 dc, 2 ch, 2 dc] into corner 2 ch space; repeat from * twice more, 1 dc into each of next 4 sts, 2 dc into same ch sp as join, 2 ch, ss to 1st dc. Break off B and turn.

Round 3: Join colour C to first dc after a 2 ch sp, 3 ch, 1 tr into 2 ch sp before join, *(miss next dc, 1 tr into next dc, 1 tr into missed dc) 3 times, miss 1 dc, 1 tr into next 2 ch sp, 1 tr into missed dc, 1 tr into next dc, 1 tr into 2 ch sp; repeat from * twice more, (miss next dc, 1 tr into next dc, 1 tr into missed dc) 3 times, miss 1 dc, 1 tr into 2 ch sp, 1 tr into missed dc, join with a ss to 3rd of 1st 3 ch. Break off C and turn.

Round 4: Join colour D to same place as joins of last round, 3 ch, 2 tr into same place as join (1 ch, 3 tr into next tr, 1 tr into next 8 tr, 3 tr into next tr) 4 times omitting 3 tr at end of last repeat, ss to 3rd of first 3 ch. Break off D and turn.

Round 5: Join colour E to first tr after next 1 ch sp. 1 dc into same place as join, 1 dc into next tr, *(1 dtr into next tr, then bending dtr in half to form bobble on RS of square, work 1 dc into next tr, 1 dc into next tr) 4 times, 3 tr into corner 1 ch sp, 1 dc into each of next 2 tr, repeat from * 3 times omitting 2 dc at end of last repeat, ss to first dc. Break off E and turn.

Round 6: Join colour F to 1st dc of any side, 3 ch (1 tr into each st to centre tr of 3 tr at corner, 3 tr into corner tr) 4 times, 1 tr in next tr, ss to 3rd of 1st 3 ch. Fasten off.

Making up

Gently press patch flat. Sew in all ends. Either sew all four sides to your garment, or sew up just three sides, leaving the top open to make a pocket.

Bobble pocket

Dare to be different with this textured, bobbly pocket. It's quick and fun to make, and ideal for spicing up a plain cardigan or sweater.

Materials

1 x 50 g (1.75 oz) ball of Sirdar Snuggly DK in Flamenco
5 mm crochet hook

Special abbreviations

Make a bobble by working tr5 tog as follows: *yrh,

Above: A textured, bobble pocket is really easy.

insert hook into st, yrh, draw through work, yrh, draw through 2 loops; repeat from * 4 times, yrh, draw through all 6 loops.

Make 27 (or any multiple of 4+3) ch.
Row 1: Miss 3 ch (count as 1 tr), 1 tr into each ch to end, turn.
Row 2: 1 ch, 1 dc into each of first 2 sts, *work tr5tog into next st, 1 dc into each of next 3 sts; repeat from * to last 3 sts, work tr5tog into next st, 1 dc into each of last 2 sts, including top of tch, turn.
Row 3: 3 ch (count as 1 tr), miss first st, 1 tr into each st to end, turn.

Row 4: 1 ch, 1 dc into each of 1st 4 sts, *work tr5tog into next st, 1 dc into each of next 3 sts; repeat from * 1 dc into top of tch, turn.
Row 5: 3 ch (count as 1 tr), miss first st, 1 tr into each st to end, turn.
Repeat rows 2–5 until you have a square. Do not fasten off.

Edging

Work 1 round of dc evenly around the edge of your pocket, working 3 dc at each corner. Join with a ss to first dc. Fasten off.

Zigzag pocket

As the pattern is quite large, it is best to use a fairly fine yarn to make the most of this two-tone zigzag pattern.

Materials

1 x 50 g (1.75 oz) ball of Rowan Cotton Glace in Shoot and Excite
3.5 mm crochet hook

Using color A make 35 ch (or any multiple of 11 + 2).
Row 1: 2 dc into 2nd ch from hook, *1 dc into each of next 4 ch, miss 2 ch, 1 dc into each of next 4 ch, 3 dc into next ch; repeat from * working only 2 dc into last ch, turn.

Above: A cool, geometric zigzag!

Row 2: 1 ch, 2 dc into 1st st, *1 dc into each of next 4 sts, miss 2 sts, 1 dc into each of next 4 sts, 3 dc into next st; repeat from * working only 2 dc into last st, turn.
Repeat row 2 twice more.
Change to colour B. Work row 2 four times. Alternating between the two colours, work five bands of colour.

Edging
Using colour B 1 ch, work 1 dc into each row end along the side of the pocket, work 1 dc into 1st ch, 1 htr into next ch, 1 tr into each of next 2 sts, 1 dtr into next ch. Work 2 dc into the side of the dtr you've just made, 1 dc into the base of the dtr. Work 1 st into the base ch as follows: *1 dc into 1st of 2 ch at point, miss 2nd of these ch, 1 dc into next ch, 1 htr into next ch, 1 tr into each of next 2 ch, 1 dtr into next ch, 1 tr into each of next 2 ch, 1 htr into next ch, 1 dc into next ch; repeat from * ending 1 dtr. Work 2 dc into the side of the dtr and 1 dc into the base of the dtr, 1 dc into each row end to top of pocket. Fasten off.

Making up
Press pocket gently and sew, crochet or stick to your clothes.

Magic garden pocket

Make an amazing realistic grass pocket using loop stitch. Cutting the fabric makes it look like blades of grass! Add a flower to complete your own miniature crochet garden!

Materials
1 x 25 g (1 oz) ball of Sirdar Bonus Toytime in Apple
1 x 25 g (1 oz) ball of Sirdar Bonus Toytime in Popsicle
5 mm crochet hook

Special abbreviation:
loop st: This is a very simple variation on double crochet. Hold the work and yarn as if to double crochet. Insert hook into work as if to dc, pick up the yarn on both sides of the loop made by your finger, and draw the 2 strands through, yrh and draw all loops through on hook.

Pocket
Using Apple, make 21 ch (or any number of sts).
Row 1: 1 dc into 2nd ch from hook and each ch to end, turn.
Row 2: 1 ch, 1 loop st into each st to end, turn.
Row 3: 1 ch, 1 dc into each st to end.
  Repeat rows 2 and 3 until pocket is 5 in (13 cm) high ending on a row 3.
Fasten off.

Now for the fun part. Take a pair of scissors and cut each of the loops in the centre to make the fabric look like grass.

Flower
Using Popsicle, make 6 ch and join in a ring with ss.
Round 1: 14 dc into ring, ss to 1st dc at beg of round to close.
Round 2: Work (1 dc, 6 ch, 1 dc) into front loop only of each dc, ss to 1st dc to close.
Round 3: Work (1 dc, 8 ch, 1 dc) into back loop only of each dc, ss to 1st dc to close.
Fasten off.

Sew flower onto grassy pocket.

project index

Here's a gallery of all the specially designed projects featured in the book. They use a range of interesting new yarns to help create a truly unique look. Once you have become familiar with the basic techniques, you'll find all these projects easy and fun to make.

  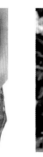 

project index

beret

Get the Parisian chic look with this classic round beret, perfect all year round. It is crocheted in a spiral using just double crochet. The variegated wool gives it a fantastic textured look.

Materials
2 x 100 g (3.5 oz) skeins of Colinette Point Five in Neptune
9 mm crochet hook

Size
Small to medium; large
Instructions for small size are given first, larger size is in brackets.

Skill
Easy

Tension
8 sts and 9 rows to 10 cm (4 in) measured over rows of dc using a 9 mm hook.

Special abbreviations
dc2tog: insert hook into next st, yarn round hook, draw through a loop, insert hook into next st, yrh, draw through a loop, yrh and draw through all 3 loops, leaving just 1 loop.

Pattern
Make 4 ch, and join into a ring with a ss.
Round 1: 1 ch, work 7 dc into the ring.
Round 2: 2 dc into each dc to end. (14 sts)
Round 3: *1 dc into next st, 2dc into next st; repeat from * to end. (21 sts).
Round 4: *1 dc into each of next 2 sts, 2dc into next st; repeat from * to end. (28 sts).

Round 5: *1 dc into each of next 3 sts, 2dc into next st; repeat from * to end. (35 sts).
Round 6: *1 dc into each of next 4 sts, 2dc into next st; repeat from * to end. (42 sts).
Round 7: 1 dc into each dc to end.
Round 8: *1 dc into each of next 5 sts, 2dc into next st; repeat from * to end. (49 sts).

Small/medium:
Rounds 9, 10 and 11: 1 dc into each dc to end.
Round 12: * 1 dc into each of next 5 dc, dc2tog; repeat from * to end. (42 sts).
Round 13: *1 dc into each of next 4 dc, dc2tog; repeat from * to end. (35 sts).
Round 14: *1 dc into each of next 3 dc, dc2tog; repeat from * to end. (28 sts).
Round 15: 1 dc into each dc. At the end of the round, join to 1st dc of previous round with a ss.
Fasten off and sew in yarn end.

Large beret:
Round 9: 1 dc into each dc to end.
Round 10: increase by 5 sts evenly over the round. (54 sts.)
Round 11: 1 dc into each dc to end.
Round 12: *1 dc into each of next 4 dc, dc2tog; repeat from * to end. (45 sts).
Round 13: *1 dc into each of next 3 dc, dc2tog; repeat from * to end. (36 sts).
Round 14: 1 dc into each dc to end.
Round 15: 1 dc into each dc to end. At the end of

the round, join to 1st dc of previous round with a ss.
Fasten off and sew in yarn end.

tips & hints
• If you need to tighten the beret to fit, thread shirring elastic around the edge.

cloche hat

This pretty cloche hat with its shell border is inspired by the 1920s. You could also add a decorative flower pin to it. The cool cotton yarn makes it perfect for spring or summer.

Materials
2 x 50g (1.25 oz) ball of Rowan All Seasons Cotton in Soul.
1 x 50 g (1.25 oz) ball of Rowan All Seasons Cotton in Jaunty.
4.5 mm crochet hook

Size
Small, medium, large

Skill
Easy

Tension
14 sts and 17 rows to 10 cm (4 in) measured over rows of dc using 4.5 mm hook.

Pattern
Make 4 ch, join into a ring with a ss.
Round 1: 8 dc into ring
Round 2: 2 dc into each dc. (16 sts)
Round 3: *1 dc into next dc, 2dc into next dc; repeat from * to end. (24 sts)
Round 4: *1 dc into each of next 2 dc, 2dc into next dc; repeat from * to end. (32 sts)
Round 5: *1 dc into each of next 3 dc, 2dc into next dc; repeat from * to end. (40 sts)
Round 6: *1 dc into each of next 4 dc, 2dc into next dc; repeat from * to end. (48 sts)
Round 7: *1 dc into each of next 5 dc, 2dc into next dc; repeat from * to end. (56 sts)

Round 8: *1 dc into each of next 6 dc, 2dc into next dc; repeat from * to end. (64 sts)
Round 9: 1 dc into each dc to end.
Round 10: *1 dc into each of next 7 dc, 2dc into next dc; repeat from * to end. (72 sts)
Round 11: 1 dc into each dc to end.

Medium and large size
Round 12: *1 dc into each of next 8 dc, 2dc into next dc; repeat from * to end. (80 sts)
Round 13: 1 dc in each dc to end.

Large size only
Round 14: *1 dc into each of next 9 dc, 2 dc into next dc; repeat from * to end. (88 sts)

All sizes
Continue to work straight until hat measures 6 3/4 in (17 cm) from crown.

Brim (instructons for larger sizes in brackets)
Next round: *1 dc into each of next 8 (9,10) dc, 2 dc in into next dc; repeat from * to end. (80, 88, 96) sts.
Next round: *1 dc into each of next 9 (10,11) dc, 2 dc in into next dc; repeat from * to end. (88, 96,104) sts.
Next round: *1 dc into each of next 10 (11, 12) dc, 2 dc into next dc; repeat from * to end. (96, 104,112) sts.

Next round: *1 dc into each of next 11 (12, 13) dc, 2 dc in into next dc; repeat from * to end. (104, 112,120) sts. Ss to 1st dc.

Shell Edging
*Miss 1 dc, 5 tr into next dc, miss 1 dc, 1 dc into next dc; repeat from * to end, ss into ss in previous round.
Fasten off.

Flower pin
Make 6 ch and join in a ring with ss.
Round 1: 14 dc into ring, ss to dc at beg of round to close.
Round 2: Work 1 petal (1 dc, 6 ch, 1 dc) into front loop only of each dc, ss to dc to close.
Round 3: Work 1 petal (1 dc, 8 ch, 1 dc) into back loop only of each dc, ss to dc to close.
Fasten off.

You can either attach a brooch pin to the back of the flower or simply use a safety pin to attach it to the hat.

russian hat

A new-look beret modelled on Russian onion domes. This unusual shape is created by varying the rate of increase as the hat grows from crown to brim. Bobbles have been incorporated into the fabric to add interest and a gold trim worked around the bottom.

Materials
2 x 100 g (3.5 oz) balls of Sirdar Denim Chunky in Ivory Cream
4.5 mm crochet hook
3 mm crochet hook
small quantity of Goldfingering yarn in gold.

Size
Small to medium, large

Skill
Easy

Tension
15 sts and 16 rows to 10 cm (4 in) measured over rows of double crochet using 4.5 mm hook.

Special abbreviations
dc2tog: insert hook into next st, yrh, draw through a loop, insert hook into next st, yrh and draw through loop, yrh and draw through all 3 loops, leaving just 1 loop.
Bobble: make a bobble by working a number of stitches into the same stitch, and joining them together at the top. In this pattern the bobble is made of 4 trebles: leaving last loop of each tr on hook work 4 tr in dc, yrh and draw through all 5 loops.

Pattern
Make 4 ch, join in a ring with a ss.
Round 1: 4 dc into ring.
Round 2: 2 dc into each dc to end. (8 sts)
Round 3: *1 dc into next dc, 2 dc into next dc; repeat from * to end. (12 sts)
Round 4: *1 dc into each of next 2 dc, 2 dc into next dc; repeat from * to end. (16 sts)
Round 5: *1 dc into each of next 3 dc, 2 dc into next dc; repeat from * to end. (20 sts)
Round 6: *1 dc into each of next 4 dc, 2 dc into next dc; repeat from * to end. (24 sts)
Round 7: *1 dc into each of next 5 dc, 2 dc into next dc; repeat from * to end. (28 sts)
Round 8: *1 dc into each of next 6 dc, 2 dc into next dc; repeat from * to end. (32 sts)
Round 9: *1 dc into each of next 7 dc, 2 dc into next dc; repeat from * to end. (36 sts)
Round 10: *1 dc into each of next 8 dc, 2 dc into next dc; repeat from * to end. (40 sts)
Round 11: *1 dc into each of next 9 dc, 2 dc into next dc; repeat from * to end. (44 sts)
Round 12: *1 dc into each of next 10 dc, 2 dc into next dc; repeat from * to end. (48 sts)
Round 13: *1 dc into each of next 11 dc, 2 dc into next dc; repeat from * to end. (52 sts)
Round 14: *1 dc into each of next 12 dc, 2 dc into next dc; repeat from * to end. (56 sts)

Bobbles
Work one bobble per round from rows 15 to 29, you should space these so that they appear evenly arranged when the hat is finished.
Round 15: *1 dc into each of next 6 dc, 2 dc into next dc; repeat from * to end. (64 sts)
Round 16: *1 dc into each of next 7 dc, 2 dc into next dc; repeat from * to end. (72 sts)
Round 17: *1 dc into each of next 8 dc, 2 dc into next dc; repeat from * to end. (80 sts)
Round 18: *1 dc into each of next 9 dc, 2 dc into next dc; repeat from * to end. (88 sts)
Round 19: *1 dc into each of next 10 dc, 2 dc into next dc; repeat from * to end. (96 sts)
Round 20: *1 dc into each of next 11 dc, 2 dc into next dc; repeat from * to end. (104 sts)

Small–medium
Rounds 21–25: Work straight without increasing.
Round 26: *1 dc into each of next 11 dc, dc2tog; repeat from * to end. (96 sts)
Round 27: *1 dc into each of next 10 dc, dc2tog; repeat from * to end. (88 sts)
Round 28: *1 dc into each of next 9 dc, dc2tog; repeat from * to end. (80 sts)
Round 29: *1 dc into each of next 8 dc, dc2tog; repeat from * to end. (72 sts)
Rounds 30–38: Work straight without decreasing. Join with a ss to first dc.
Fasten off.

Large

Round 21: *1 dc into each of next 24 dc, 2 dc into next dc; repeat from * to end. (108 sts)

Rounds 22–26: Work straight without increasing.

Round 27: *1 dc into each of next 25 dc, dc2tog; repeat from * to end. (104 sts)

Round 28: *1 dc into each of next 11 dc, dc2tog; repeat from * to end. (96 sts)

Round 29: *1 dc into each of next 10 dc, dc2tog; repeat from * to end. (88 sts)

Round 30: *1 dc into each of next 9 dc, dc2tog; repeat from * to end. (80 sts)

Rounds 31–39: Work straight without decreasing. Join with a ss to first dc.

Fasten off.

Edging

With right side facing attach gold yarn to brim, work 1 dc into each dc to end. Join with a ss to first dc.

Fasten off.

Making up

Sew in all ends.

stripy mittens

These super-chunky, stripy mittens are easy to make, with a ribbed cuff and alternating colours worked in double crochet. They will keep hands warm on the chilliest of days.

Materials
1 x 100 g (3.5 oz) ball of Sirdar Bonus Chunky in Denim (colour A)
1 x 100 g (3.5 oz) ball of Sirdar Bonus Chunky in Bluebell (colour B)
5.5 mm crochet hook
6.5 mm crochet hook
Shirring elastic

Size
Measured from wrist bone to middle finger tip:
Small: 16.5–18 cm (6 $\frac{1}{2}$–7 in)
Medium: 18–19 cm (7–7 $\frac{1}{2}$ in)
Large: 19–20.5 cm (7 $\frac{1}{2}$–8 in)
Instructions for small size are given first, larger sizes are in brackets.

Skill
Easy

Tension
11 sts and 12 rows to 10 cm (4 in) measured over rows of dc using 6.5 mm hook.

Special abbreviations
dc BLO – double crochet into the back loop only.
dc2tog: insert hook into next st, yrh, draw through a loop, insert hook into next st, yrh and draw through all 3 loops, leaving just 1 loop.

Pattern
Right mitten
Cuff
Using colour A and 5.5 mm hook, make 9 ch.
Row 1: 1 dc into 2nd ch from hook, 1 ch into each dc to end (8 sts). Turn.
Row 2: 1 ch, dc BLO into each st to end.
Repeat this row 21 (23, 25) more times.
Do not fasten off.

Join cuff by working ss into corresponding sts of last row and back of the base chain. Turn cuff inside out. This is now the right side.
Change to 6.5 mm hook and attach colour B.
Round 1: 1 ch, 1dc into each row end. Join to starting ch with a ss. (23, 25, 27) sts)
Round 2: 1 ch, 1 dc into each st to end. Join to starting ch with a ss.
Repeat round 2 three more times.
Round 6: Using colour A, 1 ch, 1 dc into first st, 5 ch to make thumbhole, miss 4 dc, 1 dc into each dc to end. Join to starting ch with a ss.
Round 7: 1 ch, 1 dc into first st, 1 dc into each ch, 1 dc into each st to end. Join to starting ch with a ss. (24, 26, 28) sts)
Rounds 8–10: 1 ch, 1 dc into each st to end. Join to starting ch with a ss.
Round 11: Using colour B, 1 ch, dc2tog, 1 dc into each of next 10 (11, 12) sts, dc2tog, 1 dc into each st to end. Join to starting ch with a ss. (22 (24, 26) sts)

Round 12: 1 ch, 1 dc into each st to end. Join to starting ch with a ss.
Round 13: 1 ch, dc2tog, 1 dc into each of next 9 (10, 11) sts, dc2tog, 1 dc into each st to end. Join to starting ch with a ss. (20 (22, 24) sts)
Round 14: 1 ch, 1 dc into each st to end. Join to starting ch with a ss.
Round 15: 1 ch, dc2tog, 1 dc into each of next 8 (9, 10) sts, dc2tog, 1 dc into each st to end. Join to starting ch with a ss. (18 (20, 22) sts)
Round 16: Using colour A, 1 ch, dc2tog, 1 dc into each of next 7 (8, 9) sts, dc2tog, 1 dc into each st to end. Join to starting ch with a ss. (16 (18, 20) sts)
Round 17: 1 ch, dc2tog, 1 dc into each of next 6 (7, 8) sts, dc2tog, 1 dc into each st to end. Join to starting ch with a ss. (14 (16, 18) sts)
Round 18: 1 ch, dc2tog, 1 dc into each of next 5 (6, 7) sts, dc2tog, 1 dc into each st to end. Join to starting ch with a ss. (12 (14, 16) sts)
Round 19: 1 ch, dc2tog, 1 dc into each of next 4 (5, 6) sts, dc2tog, 1 dc into each st to end. Join to starting ch with a ss. (10 (12, 14) sts)

Medium and large sizes only
Round 20: 1 ch, dc2tog, 1 dc into each of next 4 (5) sts, dc2tog, 1 dc into each st to end. Join to starting ch with a ss. (10 (12) sts)

Large size only

Round 21: 1 ch, dc2tog, 1 dc into each of next 4 sts, dc2tog, 1 dc into each st to end. Join to starting ch with a ss. (10 sts)

All sizes

Cut yarn leaving a tail of about 8 in (20 cm), weave yarn into each of the remaining sts round top of mitten and pull firmly to close the hole at the top, but not so firmly as to make the fabric pucker. Secure and sew in end.

Thumb

Attach colour A to thumb hole.

Round 1: 1 ch, 1 dc into each st, work 8 dc around thumb opening. Join to starting ch with a ss. (12 sts)

Round 2: 1 ch, 1 dc into each st. Join to starting ch with a ss.

Repeat round two 1 (1, 2) more times.

Next round: 1 ch, dc2tog, 1 dc into next 4 sts, dc2tog, 1 dc into each st to end. Join to starting ch with a ss. (10 sts)

Next round: 1 ch, dc2tog, 1 dc into next 3 sts, dc2tog, 1 dc into each st to end. Join to starting ch with a ss. (8 sts)

Next round: 1 ch, dc2tog, 1 dc into next 2 sts, dc2tog, 1 dc into each st at end. Join to starting ch with a ss. (6 sts)

Next round: 1 ch, 1 dc into each st to end. Join to starting ch with a ss. Fasten off, again leaving a tail of about 8 in (20 cm), weave yarn into each of the remaining sts round top of thumb and pull firmly to close the hole at the top. Secure and sew in end.

Making up

Sew in all ends. Weave several rows of shirring elastic around cuff until it is as tight as you would like it to be.

Left mitten

Work as for right mitten until the end of round 5.

Round 6: Using colour A, 1 ch, 1 dc into each of the next 18 (20, 22) dc, 5 ch to make thumbhole, miss 4 dc, 1 dc into last dc. Join to starting ch with a ss.

Round 7: 1 ch, 1 dc into each of the next 18 (20, 22) dc, 1 dc into each ch, 1 dc into last dc. Join to starting ch with a ss. (24 (26, 28) sts)

Continue to work as for right mitten.

> ### tips & hints
> •To change yarn, work the last loop of the st before you need to change yarn using the new yarn. Then you will be ready to work with the new yarn at the beginning of the next stitch.

bobble scarf

For maximum winter warmth and a cool look, this extra wide and chunky scarf with giant bobbles at either end is perfect. This is super quick to make with ultra-thick yarn and a large hook.

Materials
3 x 100 g (3.5 oz) balls of Rowan Big Wool
in Bohemian
8 mm crochet hook

Size
One size 132 x 22 cm (52 x 8³/₄ in)

Skill
Easy

Tension
8 sts and 4¹/₂ rows to 10 cm (4 in) measured over rows of trebles using 8 mm hook.

Special abbreviations
Bobble: make a bobble by working a number of stitches into the same stitch, and joining them together at the top. In this pattern the bobble is made of 5 trebles: leaving last loop of each tr on hook work 5 tr in next tr, yrh and draw through all 6 loops.

Pattern
Make 19 ch.
Row 1: (Right side), 1 tr into 4th ch from hook, 1 tr into each ch to end, turn. (17 sts)
Row 2: 1 ch, 1 dc into each of 1st 2 sts, * work bobble into next st, 1 dc into each of next 3 tr; repeat from * to last 3 sts, 1 bobble in next, 1 dc into last tr, 1 dc into top of tch, turn.
Row 3: 3 ch (count as 1 tr), miss st, 1 tr into each st to end, turn.
Row 4: 1 ch, 1 dc into each of 1st 4 sts, * work bobble into next st, 1 dc into each of next 3 tr; repeat from *, 1 dc into top of tch, turn.
Row 5: 3 ch (count as 1 tr), miss st, 1 tr into each st to end, turn.

Repeat rows 2–5 twice more.
Continue to work in tr without bobbles until scarf measures 112 cm (44 in), ending with a RS row.

Work rows 4 and 5, then rows 2 and 3. Repeat last 4 rows twice more.
Fasten off.

Making up
Gently press scarf, avoiding bobbles. Sew in all ends.

> ### tips & hints
> • As the edges of the scarf will be on show, you should avoid changing yarn at the end of a row, instead change yarn mid-row on a wrong side row. The ends can then be sewn into the fabric invisibly once the scarf is completed.

froth and frills scarf

This frilled scarf in a fluffy colour-changing yarn makes a wild and wonderful look for winter. Despite its unusual appearance, it is surprisingly easy to make – you simply increase the number of stitches in each round.

Materials
2 x 50 g (1.75) balls of Sirdar Snowflake Chunky Magic in Purple Spray
6 mm crochet hook

Size
Length: 150 cm (59 in)

Skill
Easy

Tension
The tension is not important for this project.

Pattern
Make 120 ch.
Round 1: 1 dc into 2nd ch from hook, 1 dc into each ch to last ch, 2 dc into last ch, 1 dc into the back of each ch, ss to 1st dc. (239 sts)
Round 2: 2 dc into each dc to end, ss to dc. (478 sts)
Round 3: 3 ch, 3 tr into each dc to end, ss to top of 3 ch. (1434 sts)
Fasten off.

---

tips & hints
• Working with fluffy yarn, it can sometimes be difficult to tell exactly where the stitches are. You may find it easier to feel for the stitches, rather than look for them. In this pattern it won't matter too much if you miss a stitch or work several stitches into the same stitch.

granny squares scarf

Make this striking scarf using different coloured yarns in traditional granny squares, which are then sewn together and finished with a contrasting trim.

Materials
1 x 100 g (3.5 oz) ball of Sirdar Nova Super Chunky in each of: Ivory; Damson; Pine, Taupe.
6.5 mm crochet hook

Size
One size. 14 x 163 cm ($5^1/_2$ x 64 in). You can make the scarf longer by simply adding more squares.

Skill
Medium

Tension
Tension is not important for this project. Each square should be approximately 13 cm (5 in).

Pattern
Make 12 squares using different combinations of colours. For maximum contrast keep back one of the colours in round 3 and use this as your border colour.

Using colour A, 6 ch, join into a ring with a ss.

Round 1: 3 ch (count as 1 tr), 2 tr into ring, 1 ch, work (3 tr into ring, 1 ch) 3 times, ss in top of 3 ch.
Fasten off. (12 sts)

Round 2: Join colour B to same place as ss, 3 ch (count as 1 tr), 1 tr into each of the next 2 sts. *

Work (2 tr, 1ch, 2 tr) into ch sp, 1 tr into each of next 3 sts; repeat from * twice more, work (2 tr, 1 ch, 2 tr) into last ch sp, ss into top of 3 ch.
Fasten off. (28 tr)

Round 3. Join color C to same place as ss, 3 ch, 1 tr into each of next 4 sts * work (2 tr, 1 ch, 2 tr) into ch sp, I tr into each of next 7 sts; repeat from * twice more, work (2 tr, 1 ch, 2 tr) into last ch sp, 1 tr into each of next 2 sts, ss in top of 3 ch. (44 tr)
Fasten off.

Making up
Press each square. Using colour D join the squares by inserting the needle under the first st on one side of the first square and under the corresponding st on the square you are joining to. Continue to work this way from right to left until the two squares are completely joined along one side.

When all of the squares have been joined in this way, join colour D anywhere along the scarf edge. I ch, work 1 dc into each st along the edges of the scarf and 3 dc in the 1 ch sp at each corner. Ss to starting ch.
Fasten off. Sew in all ends.

beads and tassels scarf

An elegant evening scarf made using a fine slinky yarn with beads crocheted into the fabric in a striking motif. The scarf is finished off with long beaded tassels.

Materials
1 x 50 g ball of Twilleys Silky 5 Count Black
2.5 mm crochet hook
25 g clear beads (ensure the hole is large enough to pass a threaded needle though)

Size
One size. 84 cm (33 in) excluding fringe.

Skill
Easy

Tension
26 sts and 26 rows to 10 cm (4 in) measured over rows of dc using 2.5 mm hook.

Special abbreviations
dc with bead: to work a bead into the fabric, insert hook into next stitch, move bead up yarn so it is close to the fabric, yrh, draw through a loop, yrh, draw through two loops.

Pattern
Thread 216 beads onto the yarn. You should thread all the beads you need (and a few more in case you have miscounted) as you will not be able to add more beads unless you break the yarn. Any spare beads can be discarded at the end.

Make 18 ch.
Row 1: I dc into 2nd ch from hook, 1 dc into each dc to end, 1 ch, turn. (17 sts)
Row 2: 1 dc into each dc to end. 1 ch, turn. Work 3 more rows of dc.
Row 6: 3 ch (count as 1 tr), miss 1st dc, 1 tr into each dc to end, turn.
Row 7: 3 ch, miss 1st tr, 1 tr into each tr to end, including tch, turn.
Row 8: 3 ch, miss 1st tr, 1 tr into each tr to end, including tch, 1 ch, turn.
Row 9: 1 dc into each dc to end, including tch, 1 ch, turn.
Row 10: 1 dc into each of first 7 dc, 1 dc with bead into the next 3 dc, 1 dc into each of the next 7 dc. 1 ch, turn.
Row 11: 1 dc into each dc to end, 1 ch, turn.
Row 12: 1 dc into each of 1st 5 dc, 1 dc with bead into the next 3 dc, 1 dc into next dc, 1 dc with bead into the next 3 dc, 1 dc into each of the next 5 dc, 1 ch, turn.
Row 13: 1 dc into each dc to end, 1 ch, turn.
Row 14: 1 dc into each of 1st 3 dc, 1 dc with bead into the next 3 dc, 1 dc into each of next 5 dc, 1 dc with bead into the next 3 dc, 1 dc into the last 3 dc, 1 ch, turn.
Row 15: 1 dc into each dc to end, 1 ch, turn.
Row 16: 1 dc into each of first 5 dc, 1 dc with bead into the next 3 dc, 1 dc into next dc, 1 dc with bead into the next 3 dc, 1 dc into each of the next 5 dc, 1 ch, turn.
Row 17: 1 dc into each dc to end, 1 ch, turn.
Row 18: 1 dc into each of 1st 7 dc, 1 dc with bead into the next 3 dc, 1 dc into each of the next 7 dc, 1 ch, turn.
Row 19: 1 dc into each dc to end, 1 ch, turn.
Rows 20–22: Work as rows 6–8.
Row 23: 1 dc into each dc to end, including tch. 1 ch, turn.
Rows 24–25: 1 dc into each dc to end, 1 ch, turn.
Row 26: 1 dc into each of first 6 dc, 1 dc with bead into each of next 5 dc, I dc into each of last 6 dc, 1 ch, turn.
Rows: 27–29: 1 dc into each dc to end, 1 ch, turn.
Repeat rows 6–29 seven times.
Repeat rows 6–22 once more.
Work 5 rows of dc.
Fasten off.

Making up
Tassels
Cut 34 pieces of yarn of equal length. To make one tassel, tie a knot in one end of the yarn (or a double knot depending on how large the beads are), thread 4 beads onto each tassel. Tie a knot at the other end. Using your crochet hook pull the centre of the yarn through the first stitch on the end, ensuring that you have two beads on each thread and that the threads are of equal length. Pull both ends through the loop you have just made and pull firm. Continue to work along each edge, place one tassel in each stitch. Press scarf carefully avoiding beads. Sew in all ends.

basic round bag

This basic bulb bag is very straightforward and can be whipped off in an hour or two. Once you can make this, there is no end to the variations of bag you can make using different yarns, beads, tassels, loops, textured stitches, some of which are featured later in this book.

Materials
1 x 100 g ball of Rowan Ribbon Twist in Racy
8.00 mm crochet hook

Skill
Easy

Tension
Tension is not important for this project.

Special abbreviations
dc2tog: insert hook into next st, yrh, draw through a loop, insert hook in next st, yrh and draw through a loop, yrh and draw through all 3 loops, leaving just 1 loop.

Pattern
Make 4 ch, join into a ring with a slip stitch.
Round 1: Work 8 dc into the ring.
Round 2: Work 2 dc into each st. (16 sts)
Round 3: *1 dc into next st, 2 dc into next st; repeat from * to end. (24 sts)

Continue to expand the base of the bag by increasing the number of stitches between each increase by one. E.g. **Round 4** *1 dc into each of next 2 sts, 2 dc into next st; repeat from * to end. (32 sts) While you continue to increase the same number of stitches in each row, the base will remain flat. Stop increasing, and the bag grows upwards. To create a curve in the base of the base, intersperse rows of increase with rows of straight dc, alternatively you could decrease by

only a small number of stitches per row. Both methods are shown.

If you are using a very chunky yarn, as we are here, the base will grow very quickly so at this point we slow down the rate of increase:

Round 4: 1 dc into each dc to end.
Round 5: *1 dc into each of next 2 sts, 2 dc into next st; repeat from * to end. (32 sts)
Round 6: 1 dc into each dc to end.
Round 7: Increase by only 4 sts in this round: *1 dc into each of next 7 sts, 2 dc into next st; repeat from * to end. (36 sts)

When the base is as wide as you want it, about 10 cm (4 in) in diameter, carry on crocheting one dc in each dc without increasing. Continue until the bag is almost as tall as you want it, say 10 cm (4 in) high, then to make the top narrower, decrease two or three stitches evenly over the next few rows – make sure you can still get your hand in it though!

Rounds 8–11: 1 dc into each dc to end.
Round 12: Decrease by 4 sts in this round: *1 dc into each of next 7 sts, dc2tog; repeat from * to end. (32 sts)
Round 13: *1 dc into each of next 6 sts, dc2tog; repeat from * to end. (28 sts)
Round 14: *1 dc into each of next 5 sts, dc2tog; repeat from * to end. (24 sts)
Round 15: 1 dc into each dc to end.
Round 16: *1 dc into each of next 4 sts, dc2tog;

repeat from * to end. (20 sts)
Rounds 17–20: 1 dc into each dc to end. Ss into first dc. Do not fasten off.

Strap
You can use anything as a strap: a piece of ribbon, a silver chain, or crochet a strap. To do this, the simplest method is to make a double strap.

1 dc into next st along the edge of the bag, *insert hook under left loop of the stitch you've just made, yrh and draw through a loop, yrh, draw through 2 loops; repeat from * until strap is desired length. Attach to opposite side of bag with a dc2tog.
Fasten off.

beaded evening bag

This elegant evening bag in a midnight blue shimmery yarn has a flat base and an interesting shell design, and is trimmed with a beaded edging. To finish off, a matching ribbon is threaded through the top to close.

Materials
2 balls of Rowan Lurex Shimmer in Midnight Blue
3.5 mm crochet hook
5 g of black seed beads (ensure the hole is large enough to pass a threaded needle through)
1 m (1 yd) of 1 cm (1/2 in) width dark blue velvet ribbon

Skill
Medium

Tension
20 sts and 12 rows to 10 cm (4 in) measured over rows of tr using 3.5 mm hook.

Special abbreviations
dc with bead: to work a bead into the fabric, insert hook into next st, move bead up yarn so it is close to the fabric, yrh, draw through a loop, yrh, draw through two loops.

Pattern – base
Make 6 ch, join into a ring with a ss.
Round 1: Work 12 dc into the ring, ss to first dc.
Round 2: 3 ch, 1 tr in same place as ss, 2 tr each dc, ss to top of 3 ch. (24 sts)
Round 3: 3 ch, 2 tr into next tr, *1 tr into next tr, 2 tr into next tr; repeat from * to end, ss to top of 3 ch. (36 sts)
Round 4: 3 ch, 1 tr in next tr, 2 tr in next tr, *1 tr into each of next 2 tr, 2 tr into next tr; repeat from * to end, ss to top of 3 ch. (48 sts)
Round 5: 3 ch, 1 tr in each of next 2 tr, 2 tr in next

tr, *1 tr into each of next 3 tr, 2 tr into next tr; repeat from * to end, ss to top of 3 ch. (60 sts)
Round 6: 3 ch, 1 tr in each of next 3 tr, 2 tr in next tr, *1 tr into each of next 4 tr, 2 tr into next tr; repeat from * to end, ss to top of 3 ch. (72 sts)
Round 7: 3 ch, 1 tr in each of next 4 tr, 2 tr in next tr, *1 tr into each of next 5 tr, 2 tr into next tr; repeat from * to end, ss to top of 3 ch. (84 sts)

Shell pattern
Round 8: 1 dc into each of 1st 3 sts, * 3 ch, miss 3 tr, 1 dc into each of next 3 tr; repeat from *, 3 ch, miss last 3 tr, ss into 1st dc.
Round 9: *1 dc into centre of 3 dc, 5 tr into 3 ch sp; repeat from *, ss into 1st dc.
Round 10: Ss into 1st tr, *1 dc into each of centre 3 tr, 3 ch, repeat from *, ss into 1st dc.
Repeat rounds 9 and 10 until bag measures 15 cm (6 in) high, ending with round 9.
Fasten off.

Beaded edging
Thread beads onto the yarn. It is better to thread on more that you think you will need, any extra need not be used, but if you find you don't have enough, you will need to cut the yarn and thread on more beads.
Rejoin yarn where you fastened off, but work with WS facing so that the beads are on the outside of the bag.
Next round: *1 dc into of each of next 5 tr, 1 dc with bead into dc; repeat from * to end, ss into 1st dc.

Next round: 1 dc into each of first 2 dc, *1dc with bead into next dc, 1 dc into each of next 5 dc; repeat from * ending 1 dc with bead into next dc, 1 dc into last 3 dc, ss in 1st dc. Do not fasten off.

Strap
1 dc into next st, *insert hook under left loop of last dc, yrh and draw through a loop, yrh, draw through 2 loops; repeat from * until strap is desired length. Attach to opposite side of bag with a 2dctog. Fasten off.

Making up
Thread the ribbon all the way round the top of the bag through the holes in the pattern and tie with a bow.

disco bag

An amazing loop-covered bag in an interesting bobble yarn, made in spiral rounds to create a ball shape and finished off using a pearl bead necklace as a strap.

Materials
1 x 50 g (1.75 oz) ball of Sirdar Domino in Blue
4 mm crochet hook
Shirring elastic
Pearl bead necklace

Skill
Medium

Tension
Tension is not important for this project.

Special abbreviations
loop st: This is a very simple variation on double crochet. Hold the work and yarn as if to double crochet. Insert hook into work as if to dc, pick up the yarn on both sides of the loop made by your finger and draw the 2 strands through, yrh and draw through all loops on hook.
dc2tog: insert into next st, yrh, draw through a loop, insert hook into next st, yrh, draw through a loop, yrh and draw through all 3 loops.

Pattern
Make 4 ch, join into a ring with a ss.
Round 1: Work 8 dc into the ring.
Round 2: 2 dc into each st. (16 sts)
Round 3: *1 loop into next st, 2 dc into next st; repeat from * to end. (24 sts)
Round 4: *1 loop into next st, 1 dc into next st, 2 dc into next st; repeat from * to end. (32 sts)
Round 5: *1 loop into next st, 1 dc into next st, 1 loop into next st, 2 dc into next st; repeat from * to end. (40 sts)
Round 6: *(1 loop into next st, 1 dc into next st) twice, 2 dc into next st; repeat from * to end. (48 sts)
Round 7: *(1 loop into next st, 1 dc into next st) twice, 1 loop into next st, 2 dc into next st; repeat from * to end. (56 sts)
Round 8: *(1 loop into next st, 1 dc into next st) three times, 2 dc into next st; repeat from * to end. (64 sts)
Rounds 9–18: *1 loop, 1 dc; repeat from * to end.
Round 19: *(1 loop into next st, 1 dc into next st) three times, dc2tog; repeat from * to end. (56 sts)
Round 20: *1 loop into next st, 1 dc into next st; repeat from * to end.
Round 21: *(1 loop into next st, 1 dc into next st) twice, 1 loop st, dc2tog; repeat from * to end. (48 sts)
Rounds 22 and 23: 1 loop, 1 dc; repeat from * to end.
Round 24: *(1 loop, 1 dc) twice, dc2tog; repeat from * to end. (40 sts)
Rounds 25–27: *1 loop into next st, 1 dc into next st; repeat from * to end.
Round 28: * 1 loop into next st, 1 dc into next st, 1 loop st, dc2tog; repeat from * to end. (32 sts)
Rounds 29–31: *1 loop into next st, 1 dc into next st; repeat from * to end.
Round 32: 1 dc into each dc to end. Join with a ss to first dc.
Fasten off.

Note: if you want to make the bag deeper, continue to work rows of alternating 1 loop and 1 dc until bag reaches desired length.

Making up.
Thread shirring elastic around the top of the bag – tight enough to close it, but make sure you can still fit your hand inside.

Thread the necklace through any stitch along the brim and then into a stitch on the opposite side to make a strap.

tips & hints
• Precision is not all-important when making this bag! Don't worry if you think you might have missed the odd stitch or added too many – this will not affect the overall shape of the bag and the loop surface will conceal any errors.

purse on a belt

A funky hipster belt with a wave pattern in contrasting colours, which can be worn with a matching purse that simply slides onto it.

Materials
1 x 50 g (1.75 oz) ball of Rowan
   Cotton Glace in Poppy (colour A)
1 x 50g (1.75 oz) ball of Rowan
   Cotton Glace in Bubbles (colour B)
4 mm crochet hook
Popper

Belt size
Small: 74 cm (29 in)
Medium: 81cm (32 in)
Large: 89 cm (35 in)
Instructions for small size are given first, larger sizes are in brackets.

Skill
Medium

Tension
18 sts and 22 rows measured to 10 cm (4 in) measured over rows of dc using 4 mm hook.

Special abbreviations
dtr: double treble. Yrh twice, insert the hook into next st, yrh, draw through a loop, yrh, draw through first 2 loops, yrh, draw through next 2 loops, yrh, draw through last 2 loops.
dc2tog: insert hook into next st, yrh, draw through a loop, insert hook into next st, yrh, draw through a loop, yrh and draw through all 3 loops.
dc3tog: insert hook into next st, yrh, draw through a loop, insert hook into next st, yrh, through a loop, insert hook into next st, yrh, draw through a loop, yrh, draw through all 4 loops.

Pattern – Belt
Using colour A, make 128 (142, 156) ch.
Row 1: Miss 2 ch, (count as 1 dc) *1 dc into next st, 1 htr into each of next 2 sts, 1 tr into each of next 2 sts, 1 dtr into each of next 3 sts, 1 tr into each of next 2 sts, 1 htr into each of next 2 sts, 1 dc into each of next 2 sts; repeat from * to end, turn.
Row 2: 1 ch (counts as 1 dc), miss first dc, 1 dc into each st to end including top of tch, turn.
Row 3: Change to colour B, 4 ch (count as 1 dtr), miss 1st st, * 1 dtr into next st, 1 tr into each of next 2 sts, 1 htr into each of next 2 sts, 1 dc into each of next 3 sts, 1 htr into each of next 2 sts, 1 tr into each of next 2 sts, 1 dtr into each of next 2 sts; repeat from * to end including top of tch.
Row 4: As row 2.
Row 5: Change to colour A, 1 ch (counts as 1 dc), miss 1st st, *1 dc into next st, 1 htr into each of next 2 sts, 1 tr into each of next 2 sts, 1 dtr into each of next 3 sts, 1 tr into each of next 2 sts, 1 htr into each of next 2 sts, 1 dc into each of next 2 sts; repeat from * to end including top of tch, turn.
Row 6: As row 2.

Making up
Press the belt gently. Attach hook and eye to either end. Sew these in place or use crochet ss worked into the hook and eye. Sew in all ends.

Purse
Set aside a small quantity of colour A at the beginning to make the belt attachment.

Using colour A make 22 ch.
Row 1: 1 dc into 2nd ch from hook, 1 dc into each dc to end. 1 ch, turn. (21 sts)
Row 2: 1 dc into each dc to end. 1 dc, turn.
Continue to work in dc for 27 more rows.
Row 30: 1 dc into each of next 7 dc, 1 ch, turn.
Working only these 7 sts, work 5 more rows of dc. Do not fasten off.
Using the yarn you set aside, rejoin yarn to the 8th st in row 29. Work 1 dc into each of next 7 sts. Working only these 7 sts, work 5 more rows of dc. Fasten off.
Rejoin yarn to the 15th st in row 29. Work 1 dc into each of last 7 sts.
Working only these 7 sts, work 5 more rows of dc. Fasten off.
Row 36: Beg with section with yarn attached, work 7 dc across section, 7 dc across centre section, 7 dc across side section. 1 ch, turn. (21 dc)
Work 4 more rows of dc.
Next row: Change to colour B, dc2tog, 1 dc into each dc to last 2 sts, dc2tog.
Continue to decrease 1 st at each end of each row until 3 sts remain.
Next row: dc3tog. Fasten off.

Making up
Gently press the purse. Using slip stitch sew up side seams. Attach popper to flap of purse. Sew in ends.

beach tote

This sling-strapped beach tote is made from super chunky denim yarn and is tremendously quick to crochet in tall open treble stitches. It is big enough to carry everything you need for a day lounging on the beach.

Materials
3 x 100 g (3.5 oz) balls of Sirdar Denim Ultra in Denim Blue
8 mm crochet hook

Size
One size

Skill
Easy

Tension
$6^1/_2$ sts and $4^1/_2$ rows to 10 cm (4 in) measured over rows of tr using an 8 mm hook.

Special abbreviations
tr2tog: yrh, insert hook into next st, yrh, draw loop through, yrh, draw through 2 loops on hook (leaving 2 loops), yrh, insert hook into next st, yrn, draw loop through, yrh and draw through 2 loops, yrh and draw through remaining 3 loops.

Pattern
Make 4 ch and join into a ring with a ss.
Round 1: 3 ch, 11 tr into the ring, ss to top of 3 ch.
Round 2: 3 ch, 1 tr into same place as ss, 2 tr into each st, ss to top of 3 ch. (24 sts)
Round 3: 3 ch, 1 tr into same place as ss, *1 tr into next st, 2 tr in next st; repeat from * 1 tr into last st, ss to top of 3 ch. (36 sts)
Round 4: 3 ch, 1 tr into same place as ss, *1 tr into each of next 2 sts, 2 tr into next st; repeat from *, 1 tr into each of last 2 sts, ss to top of 3 ch. (48 sts)

Round 5: 3 ch, 1 tr into same place as ss, *1 tr into each of next 3 sts, 2 tr into next st; repeat from *, 1 tr into each of last 3 sts, ss to top of 3 ch. (60 sts)
Round 6: 3 ch, 1 tr into front loop only of each tr to end, ss to top of 3 ch.
Rounds 7–10: 3 ch, 1 tr into each tr to end, ss to top of 3 ch.
Round 11: 3 ch, 1 tr into each of next 7 tr, tr 2 tog, *1 tr into each of next 8 tr, tr2tog; repeat from * to end of round, ss to top of 3 ch. (54 sts)
Round 12: 3 ch, 1 tr into each of next 6 tr, tr 2 tog, *1 tr into each of next 7 tr, tr2tog; repeat from * to end of round, ss to top of 3 ch. (48 sts).
Round 13: 3 ch, 1 tr into each of next 5 tr, tr2tog, *1 tr into each of next 6 tr, tr2tog; repeat from * to end of round, ss to top of 3 ch. (42 sts)
Round 14: 3 ch, 1 tr into each of next 4 tr, tr2tog, *1 tr into each of next 5 tr, tr2tog; repeat from * to end of round, ss to top of 3 ch. (36 sts)
Rounds 15 and 16: 3 ch, 1 tr into each st to end, ss to top of 3 ch.

Strap – side one:
Row 17: 3 ch, tr2tog, 1 tr into each of next 6 tr, tr2tog. Turn, leaving remaining sts unworked. (9 sts)
Row 18: 3 ch, miss 1st st, 1 tr into each of next 5 tr, tr2tog, turn. (7 sts)
Row 19: 3 ch, miss 1st st, 1 tr into each of next 3 tr, tr2tog, turn. (5 sts)
Rows 20–32: 3 ch, miss 1st st, 1 tr into each of next 3 tr, 1 tr into top of 3 ch.
Fasten off.

Strap – side two:
Miss 7 tr from last st worked on row 17, rejoin yarn in next st.
Repeat rows 17–32.
Fasten off.

Making up
With wrong side facing, sew ends of the strap together. Sew in all ends.

swirl bag

This super-fluffy and variegated yarn makes an amazing, textured fabric when crocheted. The bag is worked in a spiral covered in swirls of surface crochet for a truly eye-catching accessory!

Materials
2 x 100 g (3.5 oz) balls of Sirdar Snowflake Chunky Magic in Raspberry Spray
6 mm crochet hook.
1 m (1 yd) of 1 cm (1/2 in) wide pink ribbon

Skill
Medium

Tension
The tension is not important for this project.

Special abbreviations
dc2tog: insert hook into next st, yrh, draw through a loop, insert hook into next st, yrh and draw through a loop, yrh and draw through all 3 loops.

Pattern
Make 4 ch, join in a ring with a ss.
Round 1: Work 8 dc into the ring.
Round 2: 2 dc into each dc. (16 sts)
Round 3: *1 dc into next st, 2 dc into next st; repeat from * to end. (24 sts)
Round 4: * 1 dc into each of next 2 sts, 2 dc into next st; repeat from * to end. (32 sts)
Round 5: * 1 dc into each of next 3 sts, 2 dc into next st; repeat from * to end. (40 sts)
Round 6: * 1 dc into each of next 4 sts, 2 dc into next st; repeat from * to end. (48 sts)
Round 7: 1 dc into each dc to end.
Round 8: * 1 dc into each of next 5 sts, 2 dc into next st; repeat from * to end. (56 sts)
Rounds 9–12: 1 dc into each dc to end.

Round 13: *1 dc into each of next 5 sts, dc2tog; repeat from * to end. (48 sts)
Round 14: 1 dc into each dc to end.
Round 15: * 1 dc into each of next 4 sts, dc2tog; repeat from * to end. (40 sts)
Round 16 and 17: 1 dc into each dc to end.
Round 18: * 1 dc into each of next 3 sts, dc2tog; repeat from * to end. (32 sts)
Rounds 19 and 20: 1 dc in each dc to end.
Do not fasten off.
Round 21: * 1 dc into each of next 2 dc, dc2tog; repeat from * to end. (24 sts)
Rounds 22 and 23: 1 dc in each dc to end.

Surface swirls
To create the amazing whorls and swirls on this bag you will be crocheting into the surface of the bag. There is no exact science to this and every bag will be unique.

Swirl
Once you have completed the basic bag, insert your hook into any stitch in the row below the brim and make 1 dc.
Row 1: Work towards the bottom of the bag, creating a wavy line by crocheting 1 dc into the stitch above or to the left or right in the row below. When you reach the bottom, make a wide turn and work back towards the brim, ss into any dc along the brim, 1 ch, turn.
Row 2: 2dc into each dc, ss into last dc. 1 ch, turn.
Row 3: 2dc into each dc, ss into last dc. Fasten off.
Repeat the swirl twice more so that the swirls cover the surface of the bag more or less evenly.

Making up
Sew in all ends. To make the strap, attach a length of ribbon to either side of the bag opening.

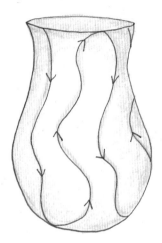

gold sparkly belt

This Goldfingering belt is the perfect way to jazz up a pair of jeans. It's made with a combination of filet and solid fabric to create an interesting stripy pattern. Make it long and wear it around the hips or short for a close-fitting, waist-cinching look.

Materials
2 x 25 g (1 oz) balls of Goldfingering yarn
  in gold
3 mm crochet hook

Size
Make to any length.

Skill
Medium

Tension
22 sts and 11 rows to 10 cm (4 in) measured of rows of trebles using 3 mm hook.

Pattern
Make 10 ch.

Row 1: 1 dc into ch from hook, 1 dc in each ch to end, turn. (9 sts)

Row 2: 1 ch, 2 dc in first dc, 1 dc into each dc to last dc, work 2 dc into last dc, turn. (11 sts).

Rows 3–6: Repeat row 2 until you have 19 sts, turn.

Row 7: 4 ch (count as 1 tr and 1 ch), miss 2 dc, 1 tr into next dc, *1 ch, miss 1 tr, 1 dc in next dc; repeat from * to end, turn.

Row 8: 4 ch (count as 1 tr and 1 ch), miss 1 ch, 1 dc into next tr, *1 ch, miss 1 ch, 1 tr in next tr; repeat from * to end, working last tr into 3rd of 4 tch, turn.

Rows 9–12: Repeat row 8.

Row 13: 3 ch, 1 tr into each ch and tr to end, working 1 tr into 3rd of 4 tch, turn.

Rows 14 and 15: 3 ch, miss tr, 1 tr into each tr to end, working 1 tr into top of tch, turn.

Row 16: 4 ch, miss 2 tr, 1 tr into next tr, *1 ch, miss 1 tr, 1 tr into next tr; repeat from * to end, working last tr into top of tch, turn.

Repeat rows 8 to 16 until belt is 10 cm (4 in) shorter than desired length, ending with a 12th row. This allows for the remaining rows, plus the fastener. Bear in mind the fabric will have a little stretch but not much.

Next row: 1 ch, 1 dc into each tr and each ch, turn. (19 sts)

Next row: dc2tog, work 1 dc into each dc to last 2 sts, dc2tog, turn.

Repeat the last row 4 more times.

Fasten off.

Making up
Work 2 dc into each row along length of belt, * crochet base of "eye" to end of belt by inserting hook through dc, then through base of "eye" and working 1 dc; repeat from * along end, 2 dc into each row along length of belt, then crochet base of "hook" to the other end of belt.

Fasten off.

Gently press the belt.

flower hipster belt

Relive the sexy 1970s with this cool hipster belt of funky flower motifs in rainbow colours. The flowers are made individually and then sewn together. It looks perfect worn with a pair of jeans.

Materials
1 x 50 g (1.75 oz) ball of Rowan Cotton Glace in each of the following colours:
Poppy, Spice, Shoot, Bubble, Sunny.
4 mm crochet hook
Large hook and eye

Size
Small: 66 cm (26 in)
Medium: 76 cm (30 in)
Large: 86 cm (34 in)

Skill
Easy

Tension
Tension is not important for this project.
Each flower should be approximately 10 cm (4 in) in diameter.

Pattern
Make 6 (7, 8) flowers in different colours.

Make 6 ch, join in a ring with a ss.
Round 1: 3 ch (count as 1 tr), 17 tr into ring, ss to top of tch.
Round 2: 1 ch, 1 dc into same place as ss, * 3 ch, miss 2 sts, 1 dc into next st; repeat from * 5 more times, omitting last dc, ss into first dc.
Round 3: 1 ch, * work (1dc, 1 htr, 3 tr, 1 htr, 1dc) into 3 ch sp, ss into next dc; repeat from * 5 more times.
Round 4: Ss into each of next 4 sts, 1 ch, 1 dc into same place as ss, * 7 ch, 1 dc into centre tr of 3;

repeat from * 5 more times, omitting 1st dc, ss to 1st dc.
Round 5: 1 ch, * work (1 dc, 2 htr, 5 tr, 2 htr, 1 dc) into next 7 ch sp; repeat from * 5 more times, ss into first dc.

Round 6: 1 ch, 1 dc into each st, ss to 1st dc. Fasten off.

Making up
Lay flowers with wrong side facing, and join with 2 slipstitches at the top of one petal on one flower to the top of another petal on the next flower. Sew

the hook/ eye onto the last flower at each end.
Sew in all ends.
Press belt gently.

---

tips & hints
• If you want to make the flowers extra firm, you can spray a little starch onto the back.

---

wrist cuff and choker

This funky, metallic wrist cuff and choker with a chequerboard pattern is super quick to make. One ball will make dozens of cuffs or chokers, so you can make them for all your friends!

Materials
1 x 25 g (1 oz) ball of Goldfingering in red
3 mm crochet hook
2 poppers for each cuff and choker

Size
One size fits all.

Skill
Easy

Tension
Tension is not important for this project

Pattern
Make 11 ch.
Row 1: 1 dc into 2nd ch from hook, 1 dc into each ch to end (10 dc), 1 ch, turn.
Row 2: 1 dc into each dc to end, turn.
Repeat row 2 four more times.

Mesh pattern
Row 1: 5 ch (count as 1 tr, 2 ch), miss 2 dc, 1 tr into each of next 2 dc, 2 ch, miss 2 dc, 1 tr into each of next 2 dc, 2 ch, miss 1 dc, 1 tr into last dc, turn.
Row 2: 3 ch (count as 1 tr), (2 tr into 2 ch sp, 2 ch, miss 2 tr) twice, 2 tr into 2 ch sp, 1 tr into centre ch of tch, turn.
Row 3: 5 ch (count as 1 tr, 2 ch), miss 3 tr, (2 tr into 2 ch sp, 2 ch, miss 2 tr) twice, 1 tr into top of tch.

Repeat rows 2 and 3 until cuff measures 14 cm (5 1/2 in) ending after row 2. If you want to make the cuff any larger than this, work a few more rows until desired length.
Next row: 1 ch, (1 dc into each of next 2 tr, 1 dc into next 2 ch) twice, 1 dc into next 2 tr, turn. (10 dc)
Work 5 rows of dc. Do not fasten off.

Edging
1 ch, work 1 round of dc working 1 dc into each dc row end, 2 dc into each tr row end and 1 ch at each corner.
Fasten off.

Making up
Sew in all ends. Press the cuff gently. Sew poppers onto each end.

Matching choker
Why not make a matching choker in the same or a different sparkly colour? The pattern is identical but a little wider.

Make 15 ch.
Row 1: 1 dc into 2nd ch from hook, 1 dc into each ch to end (14 dc), 1 ch, turn.
Row 2: 1 dc into each dc to end, turn.
Repeat row 2 four more times.

Mesh pattern
Row 1: 5 ch (count as 1tr, 2ch), miss 2 dc, (1 tr into each of next 2 dc, 2 ch, miss 2 dc) twice, 1 tr into each of next 2 dc, 2 ch, miss 1 dc, 1 tr into last dc, turn.
Row 2: 3 ch (count as 1 tr), (2tr into 2 ch sp, 2 ch, miss 2 tr) three times, 2 tr into 2 ch sp, 1 tr into centre ch of tch, turn.
Row 3: 5 ch (count as 1 tr, 2ch), miss 3 tr, (2 tr into 2 ch sp, 2 ch, miss 2 tr) three times, 1 tr into top of tch.

Repeat rows 2 and 3 until the choker measures 30 cm (12 in) ending after row 2. You may need to make the choker smaller or larger. Measure your neck and work choker until desired length. The length to the end of the mesh pattern should be exactly the same as your neck measurement.
Next row: 1 ch, (1 dc into each of next 2 tr, 1 dc into each of next 2 ch) three times, 1 dc into next 2 tr, turn.
Work 5 rows of dc.
Fasten off.

Edging
1 ch, work 1 round of dc working 1 dc into each dc row end, 2 dc into each tr row end and 1 ch at each corner.
Fasten off.

Making up
Sew in all ends. Press the choker gently. Sew poppers onto each end.

stranded choker

This sparkly choker uses strands of chains in ever-increasing lengths to create a relaxed yet elegant look.

Materials
1 x 25 g (1 oz) ball of Goldfingering in black
3 mm crochet hook
2 small black poppers

Size
One size

Skill
Easy

Pattern – Back panel One
Make 13 ch.
Row 1: 1 dc into 2nd chain from hook, 1 dc into each ch to end, turn. (12 dc)
Row 2: 1 dc into each dc to end, 1 ch, turn.
Work 7 more rows.
Fasten off.

Make another back panel as the first, but do not fasten off after row 9.
You will now be working strands of chains and attaching them alternately to back panel 1 and 2:

Strand 1: Ch 60, ss into first dc on back panel 1.
Strand 2: Ss into next dc on back panel 1, ch 62, ss into dc on back panel 2.
Strand 3: Ss into next dc on back panel 2, ch 64, ss into dc on back panel 1.

Continue in this manner increasing the number of chains between panels by two until you have worked to the end of both panels. You should have

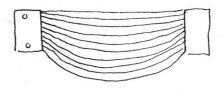

12 strands the longest being 82 chains.
Fasten off.

Making up
Gently press. Sew in all ends.
Place two poppers on each back panel to fasten.
You can vary the length of the choker depending on where you place the poppers.

> **tips & hints**
> • Take care that the strands are not twisted around one another and are hanging free before you attach them.

beaded choker

An elegant beaded choker for glamorous parties and sophisticated soirées!
Crocheting with beads adds great texture and creates a striking look.

Materials
1 x 50 g (1.75 oz) ball of Twilleys Silky 5 Count
  in Black
2 mm crochet hook
25 g of 4 mm black beads
2 small black poppers

Size
One size

Skill
Easy

Tension
30 sts and 35 rows to 10 cm (4 in) measured over
dc using a 2 mm hook.

Special abbreviations
dc with bead: to work a bead into the fabric, insert
the hook into the next st, move bead up the yarn
so it is close to the fabric, yrh, draw through a
loop, yrh, draw through two loops.

Thread 176 beads onto the yarn. Make 16 ch.
Row 1: 1 dc into 2nd ch from hook, 1 dc into each
  ch to end, 1 ch, turn. (15 sts)
Row 2: 1 dc into each dc to end. 1 ch, turn.
Repeat row 2 eight more times.
Row 11: 1 dc with bead into next dc *1 dc into
  next dc, 1 dc with bead into next dc; repeat from
  * to end, turn.
Row 12: 4 ch (count as 1 dtr), miss 1 dc, 1 dtr into
  each dc to end, turn.

Row 13: 1 ch, 1 dc with bead into next dtr *1 dc
  into next dtr, 1 dc with bead into next dtr; repeat
  from * to end including top of tch, turn.
Repeat rows 12 and 13 until choker measures 12
  in (30 cm) ending with a row 13.
Next row: 1 ch, 1 dc into each dc to end.
Work 9 more rows of dc.
Fasten off.

Making up.
Gently press the choker flat. Sew poppers onto
both ends.

fingerless gloves

These sparkly fingerless gloves don't have any fiddly shapings, just a single loop to go over your middle finger and an opening at the thumb. They are made in one piece from the wrist to the fingers with a seam at the side.

Materials
2 x 25g (1 oz) balls of Goldfingering in red
1 x 25g (1 oz) ball of Goldfingering in black
3 mm crochet hook

Size
One size – these have a little bit of stretch so should fit all hand sizes.

Skill
Easy

Tension
26 sts and 14 rows to 10 cm (4 in) measured over tr using 3 mm hook.

Special abbreviations
tr2tog: yrh, insert hook into next st, yrh, draw loop through, yrh, draw through 2 loops on hook (leaving 2 loops), yrh, insert hook into next st, yrh, draw loop through, yrh and draw through 2 loops, yrh and draw through remaining 3 loops.

Pattern
Make 2
With red, make 40 ch.
Row 1: 1 tr into 4th ch from hook, 1 tr into each ch to end. (38 sts)
Rows 2–4: 3ch (count as 1 tr), miss 1st tr, 1 tr into each tr to end, working last tr into tch.
Row 5: 3 ch, do not miss 1st tr, 1 tr into each tr to second to last st, 2 tr into last tr, tr into tch. (40 sts)
Row 6: 3ch (count as 1 tr), miss 1st tr, 1 tr into each tr to end, working last tr into tch.
Repeat rows 5 and 6 until you have 48 sts, ending on a row 5.

Next row: 1 ch, ss into each of next 8 sts, 3 ch, miss 1 tr, tr2tog, 1 tr into each of next 12 tr, tr2tog, turn.
Next row: 3 ch (count as 1 tr), miss 1st tr, tr2tog twice, 1 tr into each of next 5 tr, tr2tog twice.
Next row: 3 ch (count as 1 tr), miss 1st tr, tr2tog, 12 ch, miss next 4 tr, tr2tog.
Fasten off.

Making Up
Press gloves gently.

With fingerloop on top half, fold gloves in half widthways to form pair so that seam is on the left side for right glove and vice versa. Join 1st 5 rows of seam, leave next 7 rows of seam open for thumb, join next row.

Edging
With the right side facing, attach black to the seam at the bottom edge. Work (1 dc, 2 ch) between each tr, ss into 1st dc.
Fasten off.
Sew in all ends.

wave stripe leg warmers

These short and chic leg warmers with a wave stripe pattern and ribbed cuffs
can be worn with short skirts, over boots or even with your favourite trainers!

Materials
1 x 25 g (1 oz) ball of Sirdar Bonus Toytime DK
   in Popsicle
1 x 25 g (1 oz) ball of Sirdar Bonus Toytime DK
   in Aubergine
1 x 25 g (1 oz) ball of Sirdar Bonus Toytime DK
   in Black
4 mm crochet hook
4.5 mm crochet hook
Shirring elastic

Size
One size

Skill
Easy

Tension
16 sts and 13 rows to 10 cm (4 in) measured over
rows of wave stitch using 4.5 mm hook.

Special abbreviations
dc BLO: double crochet into the back loop only.

Pattern
Make 2 the same.

Cuff
Make 8 ch in Black using 4.00 mm hook
Row 1: 1 dc into 2nd ch from hook, 1 dc into each
   ch to end, turn. (7 dc)
Row 2: 1 ch, 1 dc BLO into each dc to end, turn.

Repeat row 2 until there are 42 rows.

To join, fold cuff in half, 1 ch, inserting hook into
the back loop only ss to base ch. Do not fasten off.

Row 1: 1 ch, 1 dc into each row end, ss to starting
   ch, turn. (42 dc)
Change to Aubergine and 4.5 mm hook.
Row 2: 1 ch, *1 dc, 1 htr, 3 tr, 1 htr, 1 dc; repeat
   from * to end, ss into 1 ch.
Row 3: As row 2.
Change to Popsicle. You can carry the first yarn on
the inside of the legwarmer as you will be needing
it again in two rows time.
Row 4: 3 ch, miss 1st dc, 1 htr, 3dc, 1htr, 1 tr, * 1
   tr, 1 htr, 3 dc, 1 htr, 1 tr; repeat from * to end, ss
   to top of 3 tch, turn.
Row 5: As row 4.
Repeat rows 2–5 three more times, repeat rows 2
   and 3.
Fasten off.

Make another cuff as the first, this time after you
have joined the side seam of the cuff, without
fastening off, ss it to the inside of the legwarmer.
Fasten off.

Making up
Sew in all ends. Weave three rows of shirring
elastic through each cuff until they are as tight as
you need.
Fasten off.

frilly mini

This is a truly frilly mini! It is made by working rows of uneven length, from one side and working to the other, to make a wrap-around hipster skirt with a wild jagged edge. A simple ribbon tie completes the look.

Materials
4 (4, 5) 50 g (1.75 oz) balls of 4 ply mohair in sky blue
4.5 mm crochet hook
1 m (1 yd) of silver ribbon

Size
Small (8–10), medium (10–12), large (12–14)
Waist measurement (actual measurement of skirt)
69 (74, 79) cm
27 (29, 31) in
Instructions for small size are given first, larger sizes are in brackets.

Skill
Medium

Tension
16 sts and 18 rows to 10 cm (4 in) measured over rows of double crochet using 4.5 mm hook.

Special abbreviations
dc2tog: insert hook into next st, yrh, draw through a loop, insert hook into next st, yrh and draw through a loop, yrh and draw through all 3 loops. For a description of how to create surface crochet, see page Cuffs and Collars page on 30.

Pattern:
Make 51 (55, 59) ch.
Row 1: (right side) 1 dc into 2nd ch from hook, 1 dc into each ch to end, 1 ch, turn. (50 (54, 58) dc)

Row 2: 2 dc into first dc, 1 dc into each dc to end, 1 ch, turn.
Row 3: 1 dc into each dc to within last dc, 2 dc into last dc, 1 ch, turn.
Repeat the last 2 rows 5 (6, 7) times. (62 (68, 74) dc)
Next row: 1 dc into each dc to end, 1 ch, turn.
Next row: 1 dc into each dc to within last dc, dc2tog, 1 ch, turn.
Next row: Dc2tog, 1 dc into each dc to end, 1 ch, turn.
Repeat the last 2 rows 3 (3, 4) times. 54 (60, 64) sts)
Work 5 rows without shaping.

Next row: 2 dc into first dc, 1 dc into each dc to end, 1 ch, turn.
Next row: 1 dc into each dc to within last dc, 2 dc into last dc, 1 ch, turn.
Next row: 1 dc into each dc to end, 1 ch, turn.
Next row: 1 dc into each dc to within last 2 dc, dc2tog, 1 ch, turn.
Next row: Dc2tog, 1 dc into each dc to end, 1 ch, turn.
Repeat the last 2 rows 6 times. (42 (48, 52) dc)

Next row: 1 dc into each dc to end, 1 ch, turn.
Next row: 2 dc into first dc, 1 dc into each dc to end, 1 ch, turn.
Next row: 1 dc into each dc to within last dc, 2 dc into last dc, 1 ch, turn.
Repeat the last 2 rows 3 (3, 4) times. (50 (56, 62) dc)
Work 5 (7, 7) rows of dc without shaping.
Next row: 1 dc into each dc to within last 2 dc, dc2tog, 1 ch, turn.

Next row: Dc2tog, 1 dc into each dc to end, 1 ch, turn.
Work 2 rows of dc without shaping.
Next row: 1 dc into each dc to within last 2 dc, dc2tog, 1 ch, turn.
Next row: Dc2tog, 1 dc into each dc to end, 1 ch, turn.
Repeat the last 2 rows 3 times. (40 (46, 52) dc)
Work 3 (5, 5) rows of dc without shaping.
Next row: 2 dc into first dc, 1 dc into each dc to end, 1 ch, turn.
Next row: 1 dc into each dc to within last dc, 2 dc into last dc, 1 ch, turn.
Work 2 rows of dc without shaping.
Next row: 2 dc into first dc, 1 dc into each dc to end, 1 ch, turn.
Next row: 1 dc into each dc to within last dc, 2 dc into last dc, 1 ch, turn. (44 (50, 56) dc)
Work 3 (5, 5) rows of dc without shaping.
Next row: 1 dc into each dc to within last 2 dc, dc2tog, 1 ch, turn.
Next row: Dc2tog, 1 dc into each dc to end, 1 ch, turn.
Repeat the last 2 rows once. (40 (46, 52) dc)
Work 1 row of dc without shaping.
Next row: 2 dc into first dc, 1 dc into each dc to end, 1 ch, turn.
Next row: 1 dc into each dc to within last dc, 2 dc into last dc, 1 ch, turn.
Repeat the last 2 rows 5 times. (52 (58, 64) dc)
Work 3 (3, 5) rows of dc without shaping.
Next row: 1 dc into each dc to within last dc, dc2tog, 1 ch, turn.

Next row: Dc2tog, 1 dc into each dc to end, 1 ch, turn.

Repeat the last 2 rows 4 times. (42 (48, 54) dc)

Work 3 rows of dc without shaping.

Next row: 2 dc into first dc, 1 dc into each dc to end, 1 ch, turn.

Next row: 1 dc into each dc to within last dc, 2 dc into last dc, 1 ch, turn.

Work 2 rows of dc without shaping.

Repeat the last 4 rows once.

Next row: 2 dc into first dc, 1 dc into each dc to end, 1 ch, turn.

Next row: 1 dc into each dc to within last dc, 2 dc in to last dc, 1 ch, turn. (48 (54, 60) dc)

Work 3 rows of dc without shaping.

Next row: 1 dc into each dc to within last 2 dc, dc2tog, 1 ch, turn.

Next row: Dc2tog, 1 dc into each dc to end, 1 ch, turn.

Work 2 rows of dc without shaping.

Repeat the last 4 rows once more. (44 (50, 56) dc)

Work 1 more row of dc without shaping.

Next row: 2 dc into first dc, 1 dc into each dc to end, 1 ch, turn.

Next row: 1 dc into each dc to within last dc, 2 dc into last dc, 1 ch, turn.

Work 4 rows of dc without shaping.

Repeat the last 6 rows once more. (48 (54, 60) dc)

Next row: 2 dc into first dc, 1 dc into each dc to end, 1 ch, turn.

Next row: 1 dc into each dc to within last dc, 2 dc into last dc, 1 ch, turn.

Work 2 (4, 4) rows of dc without shaping. (50 (56, 62) dc)

Fasten off.

Edging and Frills

Work 1 row of dc all the way along the front and bottom edges of the skirt, whilst working your way round, add the bottom upright frills.

With right side facing start at the top left hand side of the skirt, and work 2 dc into each dc all the way along the left hand side, when you reach the bottom, continue to work 2 dc into every row end and around every 10 rows work the upright frills as follows:

Using surface crochet, work 1 row of dc into each row in a wavy line (the line doesn't need to be too wavy as subsequent rows of increasing will make each line look very frilly), 1 ch, turn.

Next row: Work 2 dc into each dc of frill to end, 1 ch, turn.

Repeat the last row once more.

Next row: 3 ch, 1 tr into each dc of frill.

Continue along the bottom edge, working 2 dc into each row end until you want to place another upright frill. When you have completed the bottom edge incorporating all the upright frills, continue to work 2 dc into each row end or dc until you reach the top right hand side of skirt, 1 ch, turn.

Next row: Work 2 dc into each dc around the edges (omitting the upright frills).

Next row: 3 ch, 1 tr into each dc to end.

Fasten off.

Waistband

With right side facing, attach yarn to right side of skirt, work dc2tog into each pair of row ends. 75 (78, 82) sts.

Use surface crochet to create the detailing down from the waistband. This can be as swirly as you want to make it. Either work a continuous loop, or turn when the frond is as long as you want it to be, and work 1 dc into each dc back to the waistband. You will need to arrive back at the waistband where you left it and continue working dc2tog into row ends.

Work 8 rows of dc.

Fasten off.

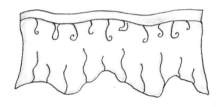

fluffy shawl

This fluffy shawl is amazingly easy to make and even easier to wear. The super fluffy yarn and open mesh pattern give this a really light feel. Wrap it around your shoulders or roll it up into a funky fluffy scarf!

Materials
3 x 50 g (1.75 oz) balls of Patons Whisper in Black
8 mm crochet hook

Size
170 x 100 cm (67 x 39 in)

Skill
Very easy

Tension
Precise tension is not important, but it should be quite loose.

Special abbreviations:
Block – mesh hole created by 2 ch sp.

Pattern
Make 136 chain very loosely
Row 1: 1 tr into 7th ch from hook, * 2 ch, miss 2 ch, 1 tr into next ch; repeat from * to end of row, 5 ch, turn. (44 blocks)
Row 2: Miss 1st tr, 1 tr into next tr, * 2 ch, 1 tr into next tr; repeat from * to within tch, 5 ch, turn. 1 block decrease at end of row.
Repeat row 2 until just one block remains. Fasten off.

Making up
Work a shell stitch border around the edge of the shawl as follows: * 1 dc into next block, 5 tr into next block; repeat from * around all 3 edges. Fasten off.

peep shoulder poncho

Crocheted in one piece so there's no sewing up, this cool poncho has cut-aways at the shoulder and very simple shaping using different length stitches to create a long tip at front and back. The poncho is finished with a long fringe of tassels.

Materials
5 (5, 6) x 100 g (3.5 oz) balls of Rowan Chunky Print in Tart
6.5 mm crochet hook
9 mm crochet hook (for tassels)

Size
Small: 76–81 cm (30–32 in) bust
Medium: 86–91 cm (34–36 in) bust
Large: 96–102 cm (38–40 in) bust
Instructions for the small size are given first, larger sizes are in brackets.

Skill
Medium

Tension
10 sts and 6 rows to 10 cm (4 in) measured over rows of trebles using 6.5 mm hook

Special abbreviations:
dtr: double treble – yrh twice, insert hook into work, yrh, draw through work, yrh, draw through first 2 loops, yrh, draw through next 2 loops, yrh, draw through last 2 loops.
Shell: work (2 dtr, 2 ch, 2 dtr) into next st.

Pattern – Front
Make 62 (66, 70) ch for neck edge, join with a ss to first ch, making sure you don't twist the base ch.
Round 1: 1 ch, 1 dc into each ch to end, ss into 1st dc, turn. (62 (66, 70) dc)
Row 2: 3 ch (count as 1 tr), * 1 tr into each of next 14 (15, 16) sts, 2 tr in next st; repeat from * once more, turn. (33 (35, 37) sts)
Row 3: 3 ch, 1 tr in 1st tr, 1 tr into each st to end, 2 tr into tch, turn.
Repeat row 3 5 (5, 6) more times until you have 45 (47, 51) sts.
Next row: 3 ch (count as 1 tr), 1 tr in 1st tr, 1 tr into each of next 15 (16, 18) sts, 1 dtr into each of next 5 sts, miss 1 tr, work 1 shell (2 dtr, 2 ch, 2 dtr) into next tr, miss 1 tr, 1 dtr into each of next 5 sts, 1 tr into each of next 15 (16, 18) sts, work 2 tr into top of 3 ch.
Fasten off.

Back
Rejoin yarn to next st of Round 1 after front.
Beg with row 2, work as Front.

Joining round
Rejoin yarn to top of 3 ch at beg of last row on front, 3 ch (count as 1 tr), 1 tr into each of next 16 (17, 19) tr, 1 dtr into each of next 6 dtr, miss 1 dtr, work 1 shell into 2 ch sp, miss 1 dtr, 1 dtr into each of next 6 dtr, 1 tr into each of next 17 (18, 20) tr, 1 tr into top of 3 ch on back, 1 tr into each of next 16 (17, 19) tr, 1 dtr into each of next 6 dtr, miss 1 dtr, work 1 shell into 2 ch sp, miss 1 dtr, 1 dtr into each of next 6 dtr, 1 tr into each of next 17 (18, 20) tr, ss to top of 3 ch.

Next round: 3 ch (count as 1 tr), 1 tr into each of next 16 (17, 19) tr, 1 dtr into each of next 7 dtr, miss 1 dtr, work 1 shell into 2 ch sp, miss 1 dtr, 1 dtr into each of next 7 dtr, 1 tr into each of next 34 (36, 40) tr, 1 dtr into each of next 7 dtr, miss 1 dtr, work 1 shell into 2 ch sp, miss 1 dtr, 1 dtr into each of next 7 dtr, 1 tr into each of next 17 (18, 20) tr, ss to top of 3 ch.
Repeat the last round, each time working 1 more dtr either side of the shell until poncho measures 21 (22, 24) in, 53 (56, 61) cm at centre front.
Fasten off.

Making up
Gently press poncho. Sew in all ends.

Tassels
Using a piece of card 18 cm (7 in) wide, wrap the yarn round the card. Cut the yarn down one side of the card so you have strands. Divide the strands into bundles of four and fold the bundle in half, draw the centre of the bundle through a stitch using the 9 mm hook and feed the ends through the loop and pull tight. Place the tassels evenly all the way around the bottom edge.

sparkly halterneck

A foxy, fluffy evening halterneck top that's super simple to make, using a shimmery yarn and worked in just one piece, which ties at the neck and the waist.

Materials
2 x 100 g (3.5 oz) balls of Sirdar Snowflake Chunky in Black Shimmer
5 mm crochet hook
1 m (1 yd) of 1 cm ($1/2$ in) wide black velvet ribbon

Size
Small: 76–81 cm (30–32 in) bust
Medium: 81–86 cm (32–34 in) bust
Large: 86–91cm (34–36 in) bust
Instructions for small size are given first, larger sizes are in brackets.

Skill
Medium

Tension
11 dc and 12 rows to 10 cm (4 in) measured over rows of dc using a 5 mm hook.

Special abbreviation
dc2tog: insert hook into next st, yrh, draw through a loop, insert hook into next st, yrh and draw through a loop, yrh and draw through all 3 loops.

Pattern
Make 68 (72, 76) ch.
Row 1: 1 dc into 2nd ch from hook, 1 dc into each ch to end, turn. (67 71, 75) dc)
Row 2: 1 ch, 1 dc into each dc to end, turn.

Row 3: 1 ch, dc2tog, 1 dc into each dc to last 2 sts, dc2tog, turn. (65 (69, 73) dc)
Continue to decrease 1 st at each end of each alternate row until 31 (35, 39) sts rem.
Work 2 rows with shaping.
Continue to decrease 1 st at each end of next and every third row until 23 (25, 29) sts rem.

Shape neck
Next row: 1 ch, dc2tog, 1 dc into each of next 4 sts, dc2tog, turn.
Next row: 1 ch, dc2tog, 1 dc into each of next 2 sts, dc2tog, turn.
Next row: 1 ch, dc2tog twice, turn.
Next row: 1 ch, dc2tog.

Neck Tie
Make the tie as follows: insert hook into far left loop of dc2tog, yrh and draw through a loop, yrh, draw through 2 loops *insert hook under left loop of the stitch you've just made, yrh and draw through a loop, yrh, draw through 2 loops; repeat from * until strap is desired length. Fasten off.

With right side facing, rejoin yarn at edge st of last row.
Next row: 1 ch, dc2tog, 1 dc into each of next 4 sts, dc2tog, turn.
Next row: 1 ch, dc2tog, 1 dc into each of next 2 sts, dc2tog, turn.

Next row: 1 ch, dc2tog twice, turn.
Next row: 1 ch, dc2tog.
Make another tie for other side.

Making up
Take a length a black ribbon and thread through bottom corners.

---

tips & hints
• Working with a fluffy yarn, especially in black, it can be quite difficult to see your stitches. Try working under a bright light and feeling for the stitches between the thumb and middle finger of your left hand.
• Take care to count your stitches regularly; fluffy wool can not be unravelled as easily as smooth wool and mistakes may be harder to rectify.
• To stop the ribbon from fraying, coat the ends neatly with a layer of clear nail varnish.

itsy bitsy bikini

For the hottest look on the beach what could be better than a crochet bikini in cool cotton with a fitted top and saucy tie bottoms!

Materials

2 x 100g (3.5 oz) balls of Sirdar Pure Cotton DK in soft green
4 mm crochet hook

Size

Small: 76–81 cm (30–32 in) bust
Medium: 81–86 cm (32–34 in) bust
Large: 86–91 cm (34–36 in) bust
Instructions for small size are given first, larger sizes are in brackets.

Skill

Medium

Tension

17 sts and 10 rows to 10 cm (4 in) measured over rows of trebles using 4 mm hook

Special abbreviation

dc2tog: insert hook into next st, yrh, draw through a loop, insert hook into next st, yrh and draw through a loop, yrh and draw through all 3 loops.

Pattern – Bikini top

Make 50 (50, 54) ch.
Row 1: 1 dc into 2nd ch from hook, 1 dc into each ch to end, turn. (49 (49, 53) dc)
Row 2: 1 ch, 1 dc into each dc to end, turn.

Small size:

Row 3: As row 2.

Medium and Large sizes:

Row 3: 1 ch, 1 dc into each of next (11, 12) dc, 3 dc into next dc, 1 dc into each of next (25, 27) dc, 3 dc into next dc, 1 dc into each of next (11, 12) dc, turn.

All sizes

Row 4: 1 ch, 1 dc into each of next 11 (12, 13) dc, 3 dc into next dc, 1 dc into each of next 25 (27, 29) dc, 3 dc into next dc, 1 dc into each of next 11 (12, 13) dc, turn.
Row 5: Ss across first 4 sts, 1 dc into each of next 2 sts, 1 htr into next st, 1 tr into each of next 5 (6, 7) sts, 3 tr into next st, 1 tr into each of next 5 (6, 7) sts, 1 htr into next st, 1 dc into each of next 2 sts, ss across next 11 sts, 1 dc into each of next 2 sts, 1 htr into next st, 1 tr into each of next 5 (6, 7) sts, 3 tr into next st, 1 tr into each of next 5 (6, 7) sts, 1 htr into next st, 1 dc into each of next 2 sts, miss last 4 sts, turn.
Row 6: 1 ch, 1 dc into each of next 2 sts, 1 htr into next st, 1 tr into each of next 6 (7, 8) sts, 3 tr into next st, 1 tr into each of next 6 (7, 8) sts, 1 htr into next st, 1 dc into each of next 2 sts, ss across next 11 sts, 1 dc into each of next 2 sts, 1 htr into next st, 1 tr into each of next 6 (7, 8) sts, 3 tr into next st, 1 tr into each of next 6 (7, 8) sts, 1 htr into next st, 1 dc into each of next 2 sts, turn.

Right cup – Small and Medium sizes:

Row 7: 1 ch, 1 dc into each of next 2 sts, 1 htr into next st, 1 tr into each of next 15 (17) sts, 1 htr into next st, 1 dc into each of next 2 sts, turn.

Right cup – Large size:

Row 7: 1 ch, 1 dc into each of next 2 sts, 1 htr into next st, 1 tr into each of next 9 sts, 3 tr into next st, 1 tr into each of next 9 sts, 1 htr into next st, 1 dc into each of next 2 sts, turn.

All sizes:

Row 8: 3 ch, 1 tr into each st to end, 1 tr into each ss in row 5, turn.
Row 9: 1 ch, dc2tog twice, 1 dc into each of next 2 sts, 1 htr into next st, 1 tr into each tr to end, work 1 tr into side of row 8, work 3 tr into side of row 7, miss 2 ss, ss into next ss at centre, turn.
Row 10: 1 ch, miss ss, 1 dc into each of next 2 sts, 1 htr into next st, 1 tr into each tr to last 5 (7, 5) sts, 1 htr into next st, 1 dc into each of next 2 sts, dc2tog once (twice, once), turn.
Row 11: 1 ch, dc2tog once (twice, once), 1 dc into each of next 2 sts, 1 htr into next st, 1 tr into each st to last 7 sts, 1 htr into next st, 1 dc into each of next 6 sts, ss into next ss at centre.
Row 12: 1 ch, miss ss, 1 dc into each of next 6 sts, 1 htr into next st, 1 tr into each st to last 5 (7, 5) sts, 1 htr into next st, 1 dc into each of next 2 sts, dc2tog once (twice, once), turn.
Row 13 and 14: Repeat rows 11 and 12.

Large size:

Repeat rows 11 and 12 once, ending ss into dc at end of row 11.

Next Row: 1 ch, 1 dc into each st to 2nd to last st, ss into last dc, turn.

All sizes:

Next Row: 1 ch, miss ss, 1 dc into each dc to end, work 1 dc into each row end.

Fasten off.

Left cup

With RS facing, rejoin yarn at left side of left cup. Work left cup as right cup, do not fasten off at the end of last row.

Shell edging

1 ch,*miss 1 dc, work 3 tr into next dc, miss 1 dc, 1 dc into next dc; repeat from * to end of left cup, ss into central ss, repeat from * to end.

Fasten off.

Straps

Join yarn at side of bikini with 1 dc *insert hook under left loop of the dc, yrh and draw through a loop, yrh, draw through 2 loops; repeat from * until strap is desired length. Repeat for the other side. Join yarn at top of cup with dc2tog, turn, 1 dc into the dc2tog, turn. Work as side strap. Repeat for other side.

Bottom

Starting at the front, make 29 (33, 37) ch.

Row 1: 1 dc into 2nd ch from hook, 1 dc into each ch to end, turn. (28 (32, 36) dc)

Row 2: dc2tog, 1 dc into each dc to to last 2 sts, dc2tog, turn.

Decrease 1 st at every row until 18 (20, 22) sts remain.

Next Row: 1 dc into each st to end, turn.

Next Row: Dec 1 st at each end of row.

Repeat last two rows 1 (2, 3) more time(s). (14 sts)

Work 3 rows straight without shaping.

Dec 1 st at each end of next and following 4th row. (10 sts)

Work 13 rows straight without shaping.

Inc 1 st at each end of next and each foll alt row until you have 20 sts.

Inc 1 st at each end of next 3 rows. (26 sts)

Inc 1 st at each end of next and foll alt rows until you have 48 (52, 56) sts.

Inc 1 st at each end of next 2 rows. (52 (56, 60) sts)

Do not fasten off.

Shell border – back

1 ch, *miss 1st dc, 3 tr into next dc, miss 1 dc, 1 dc into next dc; repeat from * to end.

Fasten off.

Shell border – front

Rejoin yarn at side edge of front, 1 ch, *miss 1st ch, 3 tr into next ch, miss 1 ch, 1 dc into next ch; repeat from * to end.

Fasten off.

Ties

Follow instructions for bikini top straps to make ties for each of the four corners of the bikini bottom.

---

tips & hints

• For more cup allowance, place the neck ties slightly off-centre, towards the outer edges of the bikini top.

index

useful addresses

UK

Colinette Yarns
Banwy Workshops
Llanfair Caereinion
Powy, Wales SY21 0SG
UK
Tel: 00 44 (0) 1938 810128
Fax: 00 44 (0) 1938 810127
www.colinette.com

Rowan Yarns
Green Mill Lane
Holmfirth
West Yorkshire
HD 2DX
Tel: 01484 681 881
www.rowanyarns.co.uk

Sirdar Spinning Ltd
Flanshaw Lane
Wakefield
West Yorkshire
WF2 9ND
UK
Tel: 01924 371501
Fax: 01924 290506
E-mail: enquiries@sirdar.co.uk
For nearest stockist email: consumer@sirdar.co.uk
www.sirdar.co.uk

Twilleys of Stamford
Roman Mill
Stamford
Lincolnshire
PE9 1BG
Tel: 01780 752661
Fax: 01780 765215

www.tbramsden.co.uk

United States

Rowan USA
4 Townsend West
Nashua
New Hampshire 03063
Tel: 603 886 5041/5043
Email: wfibers@aol.com

Unique Kolours
1428 Oak Lane
Downington
PA 19335
USA
Tel: 001 610 280 7720
Fax: 001 610 280 7701
www.uniquekolours.com

Canada

Diamond Yarn
155 Martin Ross
Unit 3
Toronto
Ontario
M3J 2L9
Canada
Tel: 001 416 7366111
Fax: 001 416 7366112
www.diamondyarn.com

Australia

Sunspun
185 Canterbury Road
Canterbury
VIC 3126
Tel: 03 9830 1609

New Zealand

Knit World
Selected branches stock Rowan yarns, phone first to
  find out.
Branches nationwide:
Auckland – 09 837 6111
Tauranga – 07 577 0797
Hastings – 06 878 0090
New Plymouth – 06 758 3171
Palmerston North – 06 356 8974
Wellington – 04 385 1918
Christchurch – 03 379 2300
Dunedin – 03 477 0400